SAXOPHONE

FOR BEGINNERS

A Comprehensive Beginner's Guide to Learn the Realms of Saxophone Basics, Music and Songs

EVERGREEN MUSIC STUDIO

Table of Contents

Introduction

"You can make a saxophone into an electric organ; you can do everything with it."

- Gerry Mulligan

More than a century ago, Adolphe Sax introduced a novel wind instrument that would change the musical world forever. Since its inception, thousands of rhythmical musical pieces and iconic songs across a wide variety of musical genres have been written using the saxophone. Its past popularity has not faded with the years, and its sound is still being used to interpret newer songs. Today, more and more people show interest in learning to play the instrument.

One of the biggest attractions the saxophone can offer the player is its great versatility. The instrument can be used to play a wide variety of pieces, and its sound has marked multiple musical genres. When we think of the saxophone, jazz comes to mind instantly. This is not surprising since the saxophone has been instrumental in the evolution of this musical genre and is emblematic and central in the most important songs of the genre. However, the saxophone has also had a strong presence in other genres, such as Blues, Soul, Folk, and

Funk, and even makes an appearance in Rock and Pop songs. As a saxophone player, this means that if you can master the saxophone, you can use your new ability to please all kinds of audiences and tastes with a variety of melodious pieces. Whether you want to play for an older group of people or a crowd of teenagers, you'll find it easy to impress your listeners either way.

Not only is the saxophone versatile in its presence in different genres, but its very essence is dynamic. What makes this instrument, so special and so appealing for new learners and saxophone fans is its great capacity to transmit emotion and message in its musicality. The saxophone can make you cry, it can make you laugh, and it can even make you dance. Its sound is sometimes melancholic, sometimes lively, sometimes thoughtful, or loving. The sound of the instrument can go from dark and dense humor to a bright, clear, and energetic one, depending on the feeling the player gives it. The magic of the saxophone lies in giving you the ability to easily switch and transition from playing sad blues songs to interpreting the tunes with the most joyous beats that make everyone dance and smile.

Since the sound of the saxophone is so unique and characteristic, it can easily make the musician stand out. In addition, the unmatched effect it can add to musical pieces has made it a timeless instrument that has already marked history and will continue to appear in songs for many more years. There is no doubt that over time the music has changed exorbitantly. However, this instrument, while classic, has been able to adapt excellently to the many changes that have come. For this reason, learning to master the saxophone continues to be a worthwhile experience, and the art of playing it is still useful and relevant.

For new apprentices, the saxophone offers endless opportunities. Its sound stands out both for soloists and in musical ensembles. As the student's learning process progresses, he or she can make the most of new knowledge and skills by delighting family and friends in solitude or even joining or forming a musical group. Those who enjoy playing music alone and who are looking for an independent hobby will find the saxophone a perfect instrument. However, those who want to integrate with other musicians and participate in musical events with more elaborate pieces will enjoy knowing that the saxophone easily integrates with other instruments and can bring vitality to almost any musical piece. The saxophone is the link between trumpets, trombones, and other instruments such as the clarinet. Extremely harmonious, it can fit into any composition.

The History of the Saxophone

Writing about an instrument like the Saxophone and especially so in a summarized fashion will always be a challenge. And not a small one at that, because despite being a relatively new instrument, the amount of information we have on the instrument from its origin to now is immense. One of the factors that should be taken into account when learning about the saxophone is its unique history, especially due to its recent rebirth. This instrument is considered one of the newer musical inventions and is less than 200 years old, which is considered very novel in comparison to other traditional instruments. Despite this fact, the saxophone has been very well received, and thanks to its great diffusion, it has reached great popularity.

Before we get started with the educational content, I find it relevant to first introduce you, briefly, to the most relevant aspects of our good friend, the saxophone.

As I have said before, my intention in this book is to try to make you, in a simple way, understand how this instrument works, and show you that you are perfectly capable of mastering this instrument when properly motivated. So, to be consistent with this philosophy, I find it pertinent to open up your knowledge by providing you some general insight into the history of the Saxophone.

The saxophone was invented by a man named Adolphe Sax, an instrument builder and clarinet player who was born in Belgium in the year 1814. This "invention," however, cannot be rightfully considered one hundred percent his own. In reality, this bright man was given a specific mission, not to create a brand new instrument, but rather to design an instrument that would be based on a previous one. His task was to produce improvement to the clarinet. He successfully completed this goal around the year 1840, when the first saxophone was created. In a way, many even consider the saxophone to be a lucky consequence of chance.

The resulting instrument received the name of the "saxophone" as a way to make reference and honor the original creator of the piece. The name itself comes from the union of the last name of the inventor, "Sax," and the suffix "fon/fono," which originates from the Greek root "phonos" and means "sound." Therefore, the word saxophone would more accurately translate to the "sound of Sax."

Besides being an instrument inventor, Sax was a musician and was also known for being somewhat of a businessman. In 1842, when he moved to Paris, he opened his own instrument workshop. There, he realized that he had not created an instrument hybrid but had managed to make a new instrument, which he later patented in 1846. After this, he focused his attention on developing many different variations of the saxophone, giving rise to different saxophone types, including the Soprano, Alto, Tenor, Baritone, and others.

With the passage of time, the instrument became widely accepted and gained special popularity in military bands. However, its introduction to the world of classical music wasn't as smooth or easy. At first, the saxophone was rejected from the orchestra because musicians believed that its sound was too hybrid and not distinctive enough to contribute to the ensemble. Its sound was often compared to a combination of instruments like the cello, the clarinet, and even the violin. This can be explained by the very nature of the instrument since the saxophone is a metal instrument that uses both a wooden component in the reed and wind to produce its sound.

Despite this original rejection by the group of traditional orchestra musicians, there were some important composers at the time, like Bizet, who was more open-minded and made an effort to welcome the saxophone better. They, unlike the others, soon began to use it in their works. Later on, circa 1870, there was an effort to create a saxophone chair at the Paris Conservatoire. This chair would be led by Sax himself, who would act as the teacher and leader. Unfortunately, due to economic constraints, the organization was short-lived and soon had to close its doors.

Many hypothesized that after this series of events, the saxophone would eventually be forgotten. Yet, as we all know, this didn't occur, and the saxophone is still a popular instrument to this day. This is largely attributed to the fact that, in the 1920s, thanks to the rise of the jazz music genre, the saxophone began to become notorious again. It was only later, until the 1940s when the saxophone was definitively added at the Paris Conservatory with Marcel Mule as the leading professor.

Over time, the versatility of the instrument allowed it not only to be used in music for military and other bands but also to grow its presence in Jazz or Classical music pieces. Eventually, it also became a part of traditional or even folk music from various regions around the world. Some of the genres in which the saxophone is widely used are jazz, both in its classic and fusion variations, as well as blues, soul, pop, rock and roll, and even Latin rhythms such as salsa, merengue, and cumbia.

The development of the saxophone would not have been possible had it not been for great interpreters who took an interest in the instrument at a time where it was expected to be forgotten and eventually disappear. Due to their creativity and passion for the instrument, its use has elevated to the highest points, and its virtuous sound has become a synonym for expressiveness in music. Today, the instrument is popular and still diversely used.

How Can You Learn To Play The Saxophone With No Prior Experience?

Some think that to learn to play an instrument, they must first be experts at reading musical language or have the innate talent of an exceptional musical genius. This myth has perpetuated musical culture. Many instrument teachers and musical coaches proclaim that to be able to play any instrument successfully, one must be supremely talented, know how to read musical scores, or have some deep knowledge and understanding of music. This idea couldn't be further from the truth. Otherwise, the learning process would be completely pointless.

Every skill in life, from the very act of talking, is something we learn and the practice to perfection. That's what learning is about, and it applies in the same way to the mastery of any musical instrument. We must study and practice in order to acquire knowledge about anything we currently don't know. Perhaps if you want to reach some level of professional musical stardom, this myth can be partially true, but for most people, those who only want to learn and enjoy an instrument as a hobby, it is not the case. In fact, I have never encountered a person, who dedicated enough time to study and practice, who wasn't able to learn to play the Saxophone, and this is taking into account that I have taught a wide variety of students from young children to elderly adults. The worst thing you can do is allow self-doubt to prevent you from accomplishing something great.

To learn to play the saxophone, you don't need to have studied another instrument before or know how to read sheet music, or even less be a genius or have an exceptional musical talent. The only things you need to succeed in this journey are a sense of hearing, functional hands, and the desire and commitment to learning.

Even then, among all these things, the most important quality that a saxophone student can have to master the saxophone successfully is passion. The overall motivation and desire to learn the instrument will be the most important factor in powering you through the learning journey. The more you want to learn it, the more dedicated you will be to reach your goal, and therefore the more likely you will be to reach it.

Finding Time to Practice

How amazing would it be if we could instantly absorb knowledge? However, this is not yet a possibility. It is undeniable that mastering the saxophone, just like any other skill, requires practice. Generally speaking, the more you practice, the better the results you will see.

You should have this concept clear in your mind when you decide to learn the saxophone or any other instrument because if you are not willing to dedicate time every week to practice the instrument, you won't be able to learn it properly. There is no shortcut to well-structured practice.

Once we've established this fact, we can begin answering other questions prospective students frequently come across. How long should you practice? How should you structure your study schedule? Should you be using any specific study techniques to make better progress? In truth, there is no straightforward answer to any of these questions. The reason that these questions are so complex is that each person has a different learning process. What someone might be able to learn in an hour, might take others 5 hours or just a few minutes.

Rather than forcing you to meet time-based standards, I always advise my students to work on an objective-based program. The important thing is to be making small advances day by day and build up your knowledge and skill progressively. At first, you can start with small goals, such as learning the different parts of the instrument and how to put them together. Next, you can work on learning to hold the instrument correctly, improving your breathing, and playing your first notes. As you conquer these small goals, you can start going after larger objectives. Overall, the most important thing is that a positive learning curve starts to form and that you tackle one challenge at a time once you master one challenge over on to another slightly more complex one.

In order to work toward these objectives, you will have to practice. In general, what I recommend for beginners is to start with shorter daily sessions. For example, you can try out dedicating about 30 minutes to an hour for 5 or 6 days every week to practicing the saxophone. The reason why I encourage students to practice so many days is that improvement requires repetition, and this frequent repetition aids memorization. Additionally, it allows you to build up your practice progressively. You will see that in any other skill, from general schooling to going to practicing a sport, those looking to see results will go for this type of schedule. This is not due to chance or a whim. The reason why this type of learning schedule is often chosen is that it is proven to work and leads to the best kind of results.

With all of this, I am not claiming previous skill, natural talent, and knowledge are not important or cannot help you become a good musician. Of course, this element can provide the student with a benefit in their musical education. Yet, if you really want to learn something, if you are really motivated, small challenges or knowledge gaps won't prevent you from reaching your goals.

In this book, you, the beginner student, will be able to acquire important knowledge about the saxophone, in a way that is especially geared for those who are just starting out or have been experimenting with the instrument for a short time. A common problem among saxophone students is that there's a more limited amount of learning resources available since it is not as widely studied as the guitar, piano, or drums. There is a lot of information on the Internet about other instruments, but there is little information about saxophones, or it is available but not complete or organized. With this guide, you will be able to learn this beautiful instrument through ordered information and selected pieces so that you do not have to search in many different places.

Chapter 1

How to Select a Beginner -Friendly Saxophone

"Setting my mind on a musical instrument was like falling in love. All the world seemed bright and changed."

- William Christopher Handy

When it comes to acquiring a saxophone, everything depends on your goals and motivations. If you want to play the saxophone like a professional, you will have to practice, and this leads us to the first recommendation, buying a good quality saxophone. If, on the contrary, what you are looking for is just dipping your toes in the water of a hobby you are mildly curious about and you do not plan to dedicate yourself to it, then renting one is the best choice. Even with renting, though, it is still recommended that you rent one of good quality that makes learning easier.

You should also take into account that the rental rates for an instrument like this are somewhat high. If you plan on continuing with your saxophone practice, in the medium and long term, rentals are not the best choice for you, price-wise. Buying a new one instead can also be pricey, but after a certain amount of monthly rental fees are paid, the expenses even out. When you are starting in the saxophone world, do not buy yourself an overly expensive instrument. The best approach is to start with one of good quality and that you can use very frequently. Over time, as you gain experience, you will discover which one can best suit your needs.

As a beginner, it is important that you don't get overly worried about the exact brand and model of saxophone you can purchase. Not being able to afford a higher quality instrument should never keep you from trying to learn. Overall, the best saxophone is the one you can buy. You don't need the best and most expensive instrument to become a saxophone player.

When you are just starting out and looking for your first saxophone, I always recommend buying the best model you can afford, within your personal economic possibilities. If your budget is not big enough to allow you to afford a saxophone of a renowned brand and superior model, do not fret. The most important thing is that you select a saxophone that works and is in good condition to play.

A decent saxophone in good condition will have a better sound and body, which in turn it will make it much easier to play. This means you will need less "air-power" to produce sound with the instrument. This is important because the less effort and trouble you have playing the instrument, the more enjoyable practicing will be. Overall, the most important thing at the beginning of your journey is that you feel good playing and feel excited about continuing with your learning journey. The more enjoyable the process is, the more likely you'll be to stick to it.

On the other hand, if you buy a sax in poor condition, producing sound with the instrument will be harder, and it will require a higher amount of effort for you to produce musical notes. This makes up for a difficult, uncomfortable, and even frustrating learning experience. It isn't hard to imagine that under these conditions, any beginner player can lose all desire to continue playing, feel like they are making little advances, and give up on the saxophone all together.

Items You Must Inspect to Evaluate the Quality of an Instrument

First of all, the metal itself, with which the instrument is made, must be inspected. Special attention must be paid to its thickness and firmness. As a basic standard, the metal must be of a composition good enough not to give way underuse or to bend easily. As incredible as it seems, there are cheap instruments made of metal so thin that it is possible to identify them only by exerting pressure with your hand. These types of instruments, although cheaper, are easily damaged and are not the best option for the apprentice. The keys must also be examined, both in their composition and in their mechanism. They must be able to be pressed properly, without deforming or jamming.

Second, it is also important to support the sense of hearing. Take special caution if you hear any squeaking or scratching when handling the instrument, especially if it is the sound of metal skimming on metal.

Equally, it is important to check first-hand the operation of the keys and their entire mechanism. The first thing is to press the keys to confirm that they are all held with the same tension. In other words, a universal force must be applied to activate the mechanism of any of the keys, without any of them feeling loose or excessively hard compared to the others. In each row, it is important to confirm that each key is at the same distance from the corresponding holes, without any of them looking misaligned. No key should be too open or closed. This is of the utmost importance since the coverage of the key on the hole has a direct relationship with the sound emission and its quality. Pressing each key confirms that there is no bounce or drag when manipulated. Any alteration in movement can indicate problems with the key's elastic and may require repair.

If you already have a basic understanding of how to play some notes on the saxophone, there is no better way to put the instrument to the test than through performance. Make sure that when you play the notes, there are no leaks in the sound. Also, check that the intonation is adequate and that the sound is uniform.

Saxophone Brands

Do saxophone brands even matter? To some degree, they do. A sax made of poor materials and cheap manufacturing cannot produce adequate sound, and its composure is usually higher. In the learning process, not only do you have to become familiar with the instrument but also with the best brands, so that you can have a reference on which to make a suitable investment. The first recommendation at this point is that you buy one at a store that is dedicated to this instrument. When you don't have access to a specialized saxophone store, you should find an advisor who is well familiar with saxophone brands that can properly guide you in your purchase.

Some of the brands that are of excellent quality, and you should keep in mind are Yamaha, Selmer, Keilwerth, and Guardala. If you are interested in a certain brand but don't have enough information to draw conclusions about its quality, then contact the store for more information and read as much as you can to learn everything about it.

Should You Buy A Second-Hand Saxophone?

When starting out, many students consider purchasing a second-hand instrument to reduce the initial costs. You can find, through a little research online or at instrument stores, very good second-hand offers. However, if you are thinking about purchasing a used sax, keep in mind that you will have to be very careful. A careful inspection of the instrument is required because there are many saxophones on sale that hide the damage. There are even some who try to sell saxophone copies or replicas of well-known brands.

To buy a second-hand saxophone, you have to be able to truly test it out and know exactly what to look for. This requires that you have a certain level of expertise and background knowledge both on the saxophone as an instrument and on the specific saxophone model and brand. If you do not know how to play at least on a basic level, you will not know if the instrument is well-calibrated and damage-free. If you don't feel equipped to evaluate all aspects that need to be taken into account in the purchase of a used instrument, this option might not be the best for you.

Antique saxophones are sometimes sold at an overly high price under the excuse that the instruments are vintage. Do not get carried away by this factor when evaluating the price of a second-hand saxophone; while an old saxophone might be unique due to its age, it will not be able to provide any functional benefits based on its antique condition. If anything, it will require more maintenance and repairs than a newer instrument. If you are considering making an investment, it is always best to go for a new instrument rather than a used old one. The new saxophones come with a front F key and a sharp F # and usually have more adjustment possibilities in the side keys to adapt them to your liking.

In short, what you should take from this is that you should only buy a second-hand saxophone if an experienced friend or even your teacher can go with you to try the instrument. Avoid buying an instrument online if you won't be able to test out the instrument firsthand. Always inspect and test the instrument or get it checked out by an experienced third party. Preferably, when buying second hand, buy an instrument from a reliable, well-known brand and verify that the instrument is genuine. At the end of the day, you will not regret taking this extra precaution since it will benefit you in your daily practice and protect your investment.

Types of Saxophones

As a total beginner to the instrument, one of the first things you must become aware of is that not all saxophones are alike. It is not uncommon for beginners to not realize this fact, and simply see someone playing the saxophone and decide they want to do it too. Yet, you can't simply grab the same saxophone and embark on your journey. To select your own saxophone, you must first become acquainted with the different types of saxophones; there are and figure out which one would be the best choice for you.

It may be difficult for you to play the saxophone if you don't have the right tools. There are four varieties of saxophone you must get to know: the Alto, Tenor, Baritone, and Soprano. With each different instrument, you'll find differences in the tone and shape of the saxophone. Basically, not only do different types of saxophones not look the same, but they also don't sound the same, and each one comes with its own set of challenges and advantages.

For this reason, you must figure out which Saxophone you need early on. Not only is this choice very important for your learning journey and can have an impact on the difficulties you experience as you learn, and making a mistake can also end up costing you a lot of money. Saxophones are not cheap. If you buy the first one you come across and end up not liking it, you will not have only lost your time but also a great amount of money.

Going forward, we'll discuss the particular characteristics of each type of saxophone to help you make up your mind on what specific instrument you would like to learn on.

Alto Saxophone

Generally, the most traditional choice for beginners and the most popular saxophone type is Alto Saxophone. I usually recommend the alto saxophone for those who are beginning to learn how to play the saxophone. This instrument can be used to interpret many different pieces, and due to its size and build, it is ideal for all, including children.

When it comes to instrument size, the Alto Saxophone is not as large or heavy when compared to a tenor sax or a baritone sax. However, the soprano saxophone does win when it comes to sizing and is smaller. Yet, the Soprano isn't considered as beginner-friendly due to certain other difficulties it offers to beginner learners, which we will explore later on. Taking all of this into account, we can consider the Alto Saxophone to be an instrument of medium size.

Due to its more manageable weight and size, the Alto Sax is highly recommended for children or younger players. Since this type of saxophone is easy to manage, learners tend to feel more comfortable when practicing and carrying the saxophone around. Larger saxophones require more physical strength to support their weight and more power to generate sound. Altogether, this characteristic can bring unnecessary challenges to the learning experience of a saxophone beginner. Overall, we want to make the learning process as seamless and enjoyable as possible, which is why we recommend these larger saxophones should be avoided, depending, of course, on the size, age, and strength of the student.

Another important aspect for students to consider when selecting a sax is its sound. You can better understand the sound of a certain saxophone by looking at the totality of the notes that the instrument can emit from the lowest to the highest. The alto saxophone has a range of notes that is ideal and wide enough to, on its own, interpret the melodies in most songs. In a way, the Alto Saxophone's sounds can adapt or mold to the human voice in a very smooth way. Overall, the Alto is a very great instrument to accompany vocals.

Due to the tone and note register of the alto saxophone, you'll be able to use it to play pieces in a wide variety of styles. Since this saxophone was created for the orchestra, it plays a very relevant role in classical music. Yet, your options aren't limited. The Alto Sax has been widely used in many other musical genres, such as jazz, pop, fusion, salsa, and many other types of music. In general, it adapts very well to nearly any song. Yet, jazz-based styles and classic pieces will offer you the perfect opportunity to stand out with its sound.

Another benefit saxophone beginners will find with Alto Saxophones is the ability to find a saxophone at a more affordable price. Since this type of Saxophone is a very popular instrument, it is widely manufactured and sold. The greater supply and demand of this instrument means there is no scarcity, which in turn, causes prices to drop. This is especially evident when compared to the pricing in more rare instruments. Nowadays, you'll be able to find good quality Alto Saxophones for very reasonable prices. Not only is this good for your pocket, but it will also benefit you by giving you a chance to purchase a better instrument, which results in a more enjoyable learning and playing experience.

If the Alto Saxophone still does not convince you, don't worry. There are three other saxophone types you can choose from if you would rather experiment with something else. However, we highly encourage you to take into account the many benefits of the Alto Sax and prioritize ease of use as you are getting started.

Tenor Saxophone

Compare to the Alto Sax, the Tenor has a more serious sound and is undoubtedly the most popular of all saxophones. Having a deep and beautifully rich sound, Tenor Saxophones have been used in many different musical styles. You can easily identify the Tenor's sound in pop, rock, jazz, Brazilian music, blues, and a lot of other songs. Like the Alto, it is also highly prevalent in classic pieces, and it has a very important role in the Classical Orchestra.

In relation to the alto saxophone, which we previously discussed, at first glance, we can immediately see that the Tenor Saxophone is larger. This instrument is also heavier, which can make it more difficult to carry and manage, which isn't ideal for beginners or younger people looking to learn to play the saxophone. Another difference can be found in the instrument's neck, which in this case, is slightly bent down. As a result, it will require more effort and air-blowing force to produce sounds and play melodies.

Those with less training or with less lung capacity can encounter more obstacles with this instrument than with the Alto. Altogether the Tenor Saxophone is not recommended as a first instrument for very young people or those with a smaller frame or weak physical constitution, as they will struggle to manipulate it.

Next, we will look at the unique sound that the tenor saxophone can produce. The tenor saxophone became a very popular instrument largely due to its peculiar sound. While the sax was originally invented to form a part of a classical orchestra, its sound quickly attracted the attention of musicians with very varied musical tastes and styles.

One of the musical genres where the Tenor Saxophone has made the most significant impact is in Jazz. In fact, its sound has even become a symbol in Jazz Culture. Its velvety sound and a great capacity for diverse musical interpretation make this specific type of saxophone a favorite among performers over the years. The deep nature of its sound is very attractive and very reminiscent of a mellow human voice. With this instrument, you can play sharp high and low notes with great results.

Another important aspect you should consider if you are looking to purchase a new practice saxophone is pricing. The prices at which you can find a Tenor Sax are very similar to those of an Alto Sax. You'll find that there is an abundance of choices available, of various brands and models.

Soprano Saxophone

The Soprano Saxophone can be divided into two types, the straight and the curved. When compared to the previously mentioned saxophones, the Soprano is considered the instrument of the greatest difficulty and is often deemed not suitable for beginners. Part of what makes this sax, so complex is its smaller reed, which requires much more air pressure and a good technique to produce the desired sounds. Additionally, the tuning of a Soprano Saxophone requires a lot of work and effort.

When you evaluate its physical characteristics, you can easily observe some differences, such as that it is much smaller than Alto and Tenor saxophones. This makes it a saxophone that is very manageable, easy to hold, and transport. While there are two versions, curved and straight, your choice will mostly depend on personal taste. Whether you choose one or the other, the sound you'll get is extremely similar. The only slight difference some experienced players notice is that at times the curved soprano saxophone may be easier to listen to, since sound travels better, resonating towards the audience through the curved path. For most people, especially saxophone beginners, the sound appears to be exactly the same.

Like the name indicates, this instrument has a characteristically high register. Its high register and its peculiar sound make the melodies played on the instrument stand out a lot. It has been widely used in ballads, and even in pop music. Some of the most popular Saxophone Soprano players interpret Jazz pieces such as Sidney Bechet and John Coltrane.

The Soprano Saxophone does have a unique sound, but playing does have to imply some technical difficulties. If you are planning to kickstart your saxophone training, you must consider these obstacles before choosing the Soprano Sax. One of the most significant issues you will face if you were to choose this type of saxophone to start playing would be the high amount of force and air required to generate sound. In the beginning, learning to control your air in such a way can prove to be a great challenge. Acquiring a good quality mouthpiece and having very well chosen and branded reeds can help you to improve this situation.

Another issue you will experience with the Soprano Sax is that you will find it takes a lot of practice and a pretty developed musical ear to get correct tuning. If you do not have a good technique, you will notice that some notes or parts of the register will sound out of tune. The only way to deal with this is by practicing and using a tuner to check the correctness of the notes.

In the long run, the soprano sax is an instrument that will give you much satisfaction if you master it. Since it is an instrument that is rarer, playing it successfully will make you stand out. However, you

24

should keep in mind that it is most commonly recommended for people with musical experience.

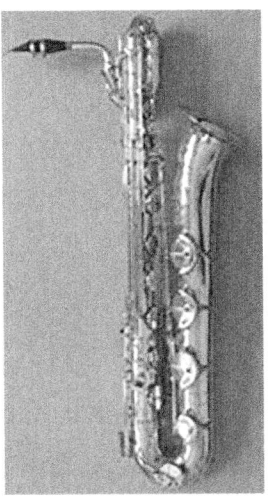

Baritone Saxophone

The Baritone Saxophone is a very peculiar instrument, especially for its large size and high price. This type of saxophone is usually significantly more expensive than the other kinds, even when it comes to the more affordable models. Due to its large size, it is generally not a good fit for everyone. Managing an instrument such as this one requires a certain level of physical force.

The Baritone Saxophone has a unique sound that is as characteristic of the instrument as its size. When played, the instrument produces deep and rich tones that can be very energetic. This instrument is capable of reaching very deep and powerful notes. That is the reason why it is used extensively in bands, especially marching bands and military bands, to support other instruments. In some styles, particularly jazz, the Baritone has also had leading roles in many melodies.

During musical interpretation, the player will have to hold the heavy instrument for long periods, which can require a lot of strength and stamina. This makes investing in the right accessories, such as a harness, of vital importance. With the support of a harness, it will be much more comfortable to have it hanging for long periods.

Another important accessory is the saxophone stand. When you are not playing, stands are great to have so that you can have somewhere to support the weight of the instrument as you rest. This will help you minimize fatigue during a musical performance. Using this type of accessories is not only important for matters of comfort, but it is also important for your health. With the right accessories, you can better prevent injuries, especially those of the back and neck.

Making A Choice

There is no definitive answer as to which type of saxophone is best. Each instrument variation comes with its own set of advantages and challenges. While some types of saxophones, like the Alto Saxophone, can definitely be considered more beginner-friendly, this is not the only consideration new students should have in mind. Sound and personal preferences are also very important, as chances are the instrument you select will remain by your side for many years to come. If you truly love or find a unique interest in a more difficult or heavy instrument, you shouldn't settle for another variation that doesn't seem fun or appealing to you. However, you should be aware of the challenges involved in more complex saxophone types so that, if you were to choose to learn this instrument, you could better prepare for possible difficulties you might encounter during your learning journey. Overall, for most beginners with no specific preferences, though, the general recommendation would be to go for a beginner-friendly saxophone, specifically the Alto Saxophone. Using an approachable saxophone like this will simplify the learning process, making it more enjoyable. At the same time, you'll have an easier time finding learning resources, both free and paid.

Chapter 2

Getting To Know The Instrument

"It's easy to play any musical instrument: all you have to do is touch the right key at the right time, and the instrument will play itself."

-Johann Sebastian Bach

The saxophone is a transposing wind instrument, like the trumpet or clarinet. This means that the music for this instrument will be recorded in the staff notation at a different pitch than that of the actual sound in which the music is played. The transposing instrument thing is a bit difficult to understand at first but to sum it up, you need to understand that your range of notes is "moved," depending on whether your instrument is lower or higher than the standard tuning of other instruments.

In order not to better illustrate this idea, for example, you should understand that the C note of your instrument is different from the C note of a guitar that is tuned in a standard way. When playing with others, you must understand these differences so that you can communicate efficiently with other musicians.

Locate The Most Important Parts of the Saxophone

Basically, the saxophone is made up of four main parts: the body, the neck, the bow, and the flared bell. Additionally, you can find smaller elements such as the mouthpiece and the reed. The saxophone is covered with tone holes as well as keys and levers the player uses to close those holes. The actual covers that seal the holes closed are called pads. Altogether these different parts and pieces interact together for one sole purpose, which is producing sound. The more familiar you are with the most important parts of the saxophone, the easier you'll find learning to play.

Saxophones come with many additional accessories, but not all of them are necessary to play it. Some of these accessories are for maintenance and cleaning. Having these types of items, such as gloves, cleaners, and rags, are helpful, but are not one hundred percent necessary.

Saxophone Reeds

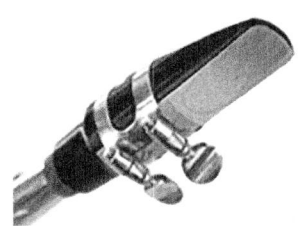 The reed is the sound-generating part of the saxophone that is attached to the mouthpiece of the instrument. This small piece is made out of shaved cane plant, so it is fully natural. For this reason, the saxophone is classified as a woodwind instrument rather than as a metal wind instrument. Due to its origin and manufacturing, you will find that each reed is unique and that selecting the right reeds for your instrument takes practice and experience.

Basically, reeds are somewhat like a whistle, when you blow into the mouthpiece, reeds vibrate, and sound is produced. The bell amplifies the sound, and this is how the characteristic sound of the saxophone is produced.

Some reeds are thinner than others, such as the number 2. The thinner reeds are ideal for beginners since causing them to vibrate will be easier. When you are a beginner, it is normal to start with soft reeds. And then with the years and with the practice, you go up. With soft reeds, the sound has a little less body, but the difference is not really apparent. As a beginner, the best thing you can do is focus on playing in tune and make getting the right notes as easily as possible for yourself. It is not convenient to force and skip the progressivity of your learning journey by jumping straight ahead to using harder reeds. You will only be creating unnecessary difficulties for yourself by doing so.

To be fully prepared for your first practice sessions, it is recommended that you purchase at least two or three reeds since these cane pieces may break or wear out. The RICO brand reeds are highly recommended for beginners. They produce good sound and are fairly easy to use.

You should keep in mind that no natural reed is made to last forever. Since they are in direct contact with airflow and the impact of sound vibrations, this piece needs frequent replacement. The more you practice and use your saxophone, the more frequent your reed replacements will have to be.

To attach a reed to the mouthpiece, you'll need to position the reed on the flat side of the mouthpiece and then set it using the ligature.

Saxophone Mouthpieces

Until now, we have talked about what the body of the saxophone is and discussed the function of reeds. Now we will talk about mouthpieces, the part of the saxophone you will be in most direct contact with. This part of the saxophone is very important and has a direct effect on how the instrument is played. For this reason, you have to take your time and choose your first mouthpiece wisely.

Each saxophone has a mouthpiece that works with a reed, which is pieces of cane that vibrate and are what produce the sound we talked about previously.

Most of these elements are made out of ebonite and are black in color. Mouthpieces can also be made out of metal. Other materials are beginning to be experimented with as well. One common mistake beginners make thinking that the ebonite mouthpieces are of poorer quality than the metallic ones. This is not the case. In fact, if you pay close attention, you can find that many famous saxophonists choose to use ebonite. Overall, the best mouthpiece for you will depend on your own personal opinion and the sound and experience you have once you experiment with both mouthpiece types.

The most important piece of advice you can follow when selecting your first mouthpiece is never to buy a mouthpiece with a high opening score. This is especially important for all beginners, since the higher the opening score is, the more force and effort that is required to produce sound. Essentially choosing a high score mouthpiece is simply complicating your learning and adding unnecessary difficulty to your practice.

Avoid skipping any steps and progress through mouthpiece scores slowly. The obstacles associated with using an inappropriate mouthpiece can easily make you feel frustrated and even cause you to give up on the instrument altogether. A beginner requires an apprentice friendly mouthpiece, preferably one with a medium opening, which makes it easy for sound to get out.

Assembling Your Instrument

If you are looking to jump straight into practice and are looking to assemble your instrument, this part of the book will provide you clear guidance for doing so.

The most important concept you should keep in mind when assembling your saxophone is that your instrument has many small and delicate parts and, therefore, should be handled with delicacy and care at all times. As you put your instrument together, make sure you are not putting excessive pressure on the neck of the saxophone or any of the smaller keys. Before assembling the saxophone, make sure there are no protectors on the neck or inside any of the other parts.

To start putting together your instrument, humidify your saxophone reeds. Since reeds are made out of cane, they can easily be permanently bent and deformed. Adding moisture to the material will make it more flexible and resistant to becoming permanently altered as it is manipulated. You can easily add moisture to a reed by placing it in your mouth. You don't have to place the entire reed in your mouth, simply humidifying one end and then the other is good enough.

Next, you will have to apply grease or oil to the area connecting the mouthpiece to the neck of the saxophone. Then you can take your humid reed and start assembling it into the mouthpiece. Examine your reed and locate its flat side. Next, do the same with your mouthpiece. Align both flat sides together. The curvier, thin end of the reed should match up with the thin part of the mouthpiece. Once set, you can slide the ligature into its spot, passing over the reed, with its widest part going through first. Finally, you'll be able to adjust the ligature until the reed is set correctly.

Once your mouthpiece and reed are assembled, continue by sliding the mouthpiece into the neck of the saxophone. You might struggle to get the mouthpiece to slide down. In this case, avoid using grease for lubrication or making any rough movements. Instead, just carefully clean the surfaces and try again.

The next step is getting the neck of the saxophone and its body assembled. As you manipulate the body of the saxophone, make sure to hold it by the bell to avoid damaging any of the more delicate components located in this part of the instrument. Take care not to force the neck onto the union with the body and adjust carefully. Finally, put on the Saxophone's neck strap and place the hook facing forward. Locate the little hook located in the back of the saxophone's body and attach it to the neck strap.

When you assemble a saxophone, it is normal for the mechanism to become clogged. This is because there are many mechanical parts in its structure. You should be careful about that fact when assembling it. Avoid pressing on any unnecessary levers, buttons, or any small components. Also, pay special attention to make sure that the octave button closes correctly. Keep in mind that you can find delicate mechanisms between the neck and the body. For this reason, you should assemble all parts with caution.

The Saxophone's Sound

Human beings are instantly attracted to sound. Even at birth, after leaving the womb, the sound is the first contact we have with the outside world. As we develop, we start showing an attraction for voices and very early on an affinity for music. For this reason, the musician has the very important task of using sound in many different ways to approach an audience in a way that communicates both beauty and message. The more skilled a musician is, the better his reach is over the audience, and the better he will be at communicating feelings and messages through abstract sound. This is the reason why, even in acoustic pieces, for example, listeners can empathize with the musician's feelings and share warmth, happiness, or melancholy. At the same time, we also perceive the sound of music as a piece of art and, overall, a representation of beauty.

This leads to the next question, "What makes sound beautiful?" This is a hard question to answer, especially taking into consideration that beauty is a very subjective concept that varies greatly according to individual perception. In this day and age, music styles and genres are so varied that the definition of "good music" or the "most beautiful sound" is completely relative and can vary according to age, social status, culture, language, and many other factors.

Ask yourself, "What kind of music is the most beautiful to you?" Chances are your answer will vary in comparison to one of the others, you know. This is why it can be challenging for musicians to strive for beauty in their interpretation since the concept of beauty itself is so hard to define.

For this reason, it is important that the musician not only thinks about the beauty of their music but also about the precision of the sound. The sound of the instrument and its different notes can be evaluated and improved in a more realistic way than musical beauty can. To do so, we must carefully study the different sounds that the saxophone produces, the different mechanisms involved in their production, and the methods we can use to develop, improve and highlight the quality of those sounds.

Producing high-quality sound should be the main priority of the saxophone player during his quest for excellence. Even as you are first starting out, it is important that you start becoming aware of the importance of sound and try to build a good foundation on sound emission. In this section, we'll explore some basic considerations to keep in mind about the qualities of the saxophone's sound.

As we will talk about more in detail later on when we talk about breathing, we must first understand that the fundamental principle in the sound of the saxophone is air. Without air, no sound would ever be able to originate from this device. The air column on its own is responsible for activating diverse mechanisms that create sound vibrations and provide the saxophone its function.

After a breathing cycle is finished, the air we exhale travels from our body to the mouthpiece of the saxophone and then passes through the instrument, causing vibrations to occur. The air column is then divided, and air travels into several sections and compartments of the inner working of the instrument. Those sections have different wavelengths, and the shortest are the ones we know as harmonics. The variation in the vibration of the air inside the instrument's body is what facilitates the mixing of the harmonics. This is how we can distinguish the differences between unique sounds and, in addition, can evaluate the sound quality of them.

Now, we must understand that these vibratory movements, caused by the air column moving inside the instrument, are not random. They completely depend on the saxophonist's breathing and their mouth positioning technique, in addition to other very important elements such as reed and mouthpiece selection.

We must also clarify that precise production of sound requires the use of a special technique that makes it possible for you to adapt these sounds to different musical genres, without having to change your mouthpiece or reed. Developing this type of skill can take a significant amount of time, and requires not only mastery of aspects related to sound emission, but also playing experience and a higher degree of musical hearing.

If at this point you don't feel fully equipped to perfect your sound quality, do not worry. Like everything else in life, developing the necessary skills to improve the sound of your saxophone methodically will involve a slow learning process. You must be prepared to practice patience and make some mistakes until you get to the point where you can fully tailor each sound to a perfect execution.

There are many aspects you should consider to develop the necessary skill to improve your saxophone's sound. The first three aspects, which are of high importance, are, as mentioned previously, our breathing, reeds, and mouthpieces. However, other factors also participate in the production of sound, and that should be taken into consideration for the best results. One element you should be aware of is your abdomen. As you play the saxophone, remember always to keep your abdomen expanded. This expansion can be seen when your belly is inflated. Doing so will allow the air to come out with more body and volume.

Muscle relaxation is another very important element you shouldn't overlook. Avoid keeping excessive tension in your chest, shoulders, throat, and or mouth. When these areas are tense, the air and its movement are constrained, and sound might suffer as a result. By keeping these areas relaxed, you will allow the air to flow more uniformly and unhindered throughout your body and the instrument. Pay close attention to your throat and verify that its position is always open. You can work on this by keeping the palate elevated. In simpler terms, strive to maintain the throat position you would while in the middle of a yawn.

Where reeds and mouthpieces are concerned, you must verify that both are in good condition. The reed should not have been subjected to a lot of previous use, nor should it be broken or damaged in any away. Additionally, you should select a reed that can provide suitable hardness for you according to your experience and skill. For most saxophone players, I suggest playing with a number 2 or 2 and a half reed. As for the mouthpiece, it must be of adequate quality and not broken or damaged. For those that are just starting to play, I also suggest not using the metal kind of mouthpieces at first.

The instrument itself is also very important for sound quality. Producing good quality sound with a saxophone is a hundred percent dependent on whether the instrument is in optimal condition. If your instrument is damaged or worn out in any way, even if you have perfected all the other elements, the sound won't be good or precise. An instrument in poor condition can cause a lot of frustration as far as its interpretation is concerned and keep you from seeing any improvements in your practice. Make sure you buy a Saxophone that is in good condition and one that has good physical characteristics. In addition, once you have purchased an instrument, you will need to follow some tips and recommendations to care for the saxophone properly. Doing so will guarantee your sax will have a longer duration and preserve its good function. Later on, in this book, we will go into detail into specific maintenance actions you can take for this purpose.

Chapter 3

Basics For Playing The Saxophone

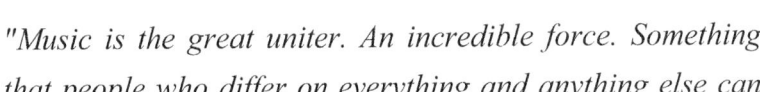

"Music is the great uniter. An incredible force. Something that people who differ on everything and anything else can have in common."

— Sarah Dessen

The first thing you should master when it comes to the saxophone is the position. The position to play the saxophone is standing, with the legs placed slightly apart, with the head and body straight. Your stomach should be slightly engaged and your chest slightly forward, as to improve your breathing and give your lungs more room to expand.

Since saxophones are heavy, some more than others, a strap is used to help with support. Neck-straps should be adjusted so that when the player is in playing position, the mouthpiece of the instrument is naturally at the level of the mouth. As you play, the elbows should moderately apart from the body, giving your hands enough room to maneuver.

The Saxophone is generally supported by three elements, the first being a neck strap. Additionally, it is held between your teeth, as they hold onto the mouthpiece and by your dominant hand, which will support the instrument as you play. You must also pay close attention to your posture since holding and playing this heavy instrument can cause you discomfort and pain. Over time, having the wrong posture can even lead to neck and back injuries.

To get started, learn to hold the saxophone correctly. The dominant hand should go at the bottom of the saxophone, trying to keep the fingers on the three white buttons. The thumb should be resting against the support. The other hand should go on top of the saxophone; try to keep your thumb on the thumb rest and your fingers on the three large buttons on top.

At the top of the instrument, you will normally be able to locate five buttons. The fingers should be supported on the largest one. You must also be able to reach the bottom that is located highest up on the instrument, which you can recognize since it is often smaller than the rest. Next, hold the saxophone close to your body. This will help you have more control as you play. To develop dexterity and skill, practice stretching your fingers towards the other buttons. This will help you further down the road since your fingers will already be used to the movements.

Next, you should concentrate on your mouth's placement and position. You should bring your mouth closer to the mouthpiece so that your teeth are close to the top of it. You should also wrap the lower lip around the mouthpiece. To achieve the best sound, you must ensure that your lips are sealed against the mouthpiece, so that no air can escape when blowing.

Saxophone Study Techniques

At first, being a beginner rather than an advanced student can appear to have more downsides than benefits. However, beginners have one of the greatest advantages that a saxophone player can have; a blank slate. At this early stage, the student is not yet contaminated with bad habits and hasn't yet developed issues or shortcomings. With an entire learning journey ahead of you, you have the amazing possibility of starting the study of the instrument on the right foot. Rather than having to work through problem areas and shortcomings, you can start developing good study techniques from day one and become a great musician in half the time.

It doesn't matter whether you are interested in the saxophone because you want to dedicate your life to a musical profession or if you simply want to learn to play to cultivate a hobby. Kickstarting your learning with the right information and the proper methodology is key to see quick improvement and good results. As a student, you will soon discover that seeing yourself progress and grow as a saxophonist is the greatest motivator you can have during your musical learning journey.

In my years of studying and practicing the saxophone, I have learned many things about how people tackle the process of learning the instrument. Unfortunately, I have witnessed many students get lost as a result of an unfocused study approach and unstructured study plan.

One of the biggest myths I see novice students fall for is that "the more hours you study, the better saxophonist you will be." It is like thinking that by lifting weights for eight hours in a row every day, you will instantly become more muscular. This type of simple myth or misguided advice can negatively impact students and discourage them from persevering in their journey.

Don't get me wrong; getting enough practice is important, but it is not the be-all and end-all of saxophone mastery. While practicing enough is important, how you study is far more important than how long you study for. After all, one hour a day of super-focused structured and progressive study is far superior to 5 hours a day of disorganized practice. Smart studying is the secret of advanced instrument learning.

If you have already started practicing, it is not yet too late to refocus your saxophone practice. At first, it might seem counterintuitive to shave hours off of your time-intensive study regime, but trust me, you will see far better results by reorganizing your practice. You will also be less stressed out and be able to enjoy more rest time. By correcting your learning approach, you are going to start seeing results faster and without experiencing study exhaustion.

Lastly, I want to clarify that I am not opposing dedicating time to the study of the instrument. Studying is absolutely instrumental to your progress as a saxophonist. What I am saying is that study hours can easily be wasted if you are not dedicating your effort to the right tasks. Avoid mindlessly repeating notes day in and day out. Instead, focus on developing skills such as the improvement of finger agility, breathing capacity, and rhythm. These are more substantial and transcendental elements in the development and execution of the saxophone.

Hearing, memory, deduction, creativity, and musical analysis are the most important abilities for any musician. It is this set of elements that will help you advance your level of performance skill and knowledge as a saxophone player. Repeating a scale or other exercise for hours on end until you are tired of it will not do you much good in comparison.

When I started studying the saxophone, I used to spend hours a day locked in a tiny windowless room, hoping to one day become an outstanding saxophonist. Even though I was incredibly disciplined and motivated, in reality, I saw very little progress in those first years.

It was only after I met a fellow saxophone student, who had only started playing a few months back, that I began questioning myself and my study methods. This fellow saxophonist was able to interpret musical pieces that took me years to work through, with less than half of the study experience and invested study hours. In theory, I was working harder, so I should be the one experiencing the most progress in my performance. On the contrary, this newer student was the one making impressive advances. Unlike me, this other student studied fewer hours. Also, unlike me, his practice time focused not only on exercises but on musical theory, breathing, and more, all according to a well-designed schedule. At that point, I understood that there was something wrong with my study approach and that my study focus needed to change if I wanted to start seeing better results with the saxophone.

Once I came upon this realization, I hired a saxophone instructor who was able to guide me more appropriately during the first stages. He designed a better study plan for me to follow, one that was progressive, structured, and could help me improve in all the elements a good saxophonist must focus on. The whole process led me to experience great results. Even if it did feel as if I was relearning the instrument, I did not care. In that one year of my new way of studying, I saw more progress than during the previous three years.

Completely turning my study method around did take effort, but it was well worth it. I no longer spent endless hours studying every day. Just by dedicating up to two hours a day of well conscious and applied for work, my progress skyrocketed. Not only that, but I also had more rest, which gave me more time to cultivate other relationships and other hobbies. You'll see that becoming a good saxophonist doesn't imply that you have to neglect people you love, responsibilities, or other interests.

I'm sure by now you will agree with me that the most important thing in learning something new is focused practice. In fact, a renowned psychologist, Dr. Anders Ericsson, has even gone as far as to claim that one person needs to practice something for at least 10,000 hours or its equivalent in years in order to learn the given discipline, art, or skill at the most advanced or expert level. This concept has been better known as the ten-year or ten thousand hour rule.

The higher your ambitions are, the more you will need to invest time and effort to accomplish them. Of course, one must keep in mind that the average student is hardly ever interested in developing the discipline and art of the saxophone to its highest level. For most, learning to play songs correctly and produce a sound that is pleasant for others is more than enough. Nonetheless, you must not forget that there are no easy solutions in music and that your progress will always be a direct reflection of your effort. If you want to learn to play the saxophone, you must practice, and you must do so in a smart, directed, and frequent way. To be honest, my experience and observation of fellow saxophonists have taught me that you don't need to study for 10,000 hours or other extraordinary amounts of time to see results. You simply have to be invested, perseverant, and follow a learning plan.

In this section of the book, I want to dive deeper into the subject of study, but more specifically on how you should administrate your study time and study sessions.

After all, study should never be measured solely in time. Instead, each study session is made up of learning objectives, measurable outcomes, and different study techniques. At the end of the day, it is only the results that truly matter. As the famous pianist Arthur Rubinstein once said, "If you need to practice more than four hours a day, surely you are doing it wrong."

General Guideless For Study Session Structure

The general structure of any saxophone practice session should be focused on optimizing your learning processes and skill development. After many years of playing and studying the saxophone, I came up with a system that works for me. I have decided to share that system with you in this chapter to help you refine your own study methodology, according to your needs and goals. In my case, I found that adhering to the following guidelines was the most effective way to see a massive increase in my progress. Once I started teaching, I passed this system on to my students and even implemented it during lessons. To my surprise, I discovered that the system I had devised for myself, with the help of other mentors, also worked amazingly for my pupils.

The first aspect that I take into account the structure of my study sessions is the student's learning goals. Every exercise or activity you take part in must be geared towards helping you reach a specific learning objective. Therefore you must figure out what you're learning objectives are in a very specific way. I am not talking about objectives such as "learning to play the saxophone." This is too general and would not help you, in any way, to structure your practice sessions. Instead, chose specific learning objectives such as "learn to play the C note" or "increase air inhalation capacity."

Divide and conquer. That is the secret to tackling such a big task, such as learning the saxophone. Find out what your specific objectives are and list them out. Then you can find the appropriate exercises to work towards those objectives. Once you start meeting your first objectives, new challenges and goals will arise, and you can progressively build up your practice. Always be clear about what you want to achieve with your time.

The second concept that I like to share with my students and that plays a key role in each one of my practice sessions is intention. You should never play the saxophone routinely. Every single note you play should be played with intention and awareness.

It is preferable to study for a short time but with great concentration than to study for a long time while your mind is somewhere else. Every time you set out, learn a new song or practice an exercise or note scale, approach the task in a focused way. Stat by carefully observing the music sheet. Try to understand what you see mentally (here is where learning to read musical language comes in handy) and be aware. Identify the different notes. Then observe the different movements of the melody as this will help you to know what the breathing challenges of the exercise or music piece will be. Take note of the rhythm, the harmony, and even the feeling behind the passage you will study. This will help you become a better performer and later on, even a better improviser.

If you don't understand or don't know something, take note of your questions in a piece of paper and look for the answers. If you have an instructor available, you can always ask for help. If not, books, fellow players, and the Internet will be your best friends.

Firstly, let's talk about the approach I recommend for learning a musical piece or song. Initially, I like to look at the composer's name and find out more information about their musical style and the period to which the piece belongs. I even like to go as far as to look into the meaning of the title and learn about the type of audience that listened to the piece at the time of its creation. The more you understand the background around the music, the better you will be able to understand the piece and what it represents. This will allow us to interpret it better and perform the piece for an audience. As a general rule, I never play a song that I know nothing about.

The time for research doesn't stop with the history. You should also perform a more technical but equally detailed analysis of the piece. Look at the tune, the notes, the rhythm, the speed, and any other indications of how the song should be played that you are able to find on the sheet music. In short, analyze the work completely.

Once you have done this, you can start to practice playing the piece. It is important that from the very first time you play a song or part of a song, you are aware and respectful of all the indications written in the music sheet. Even if you are going slowly, take note of the sound effects that are used, the dynamics of the piece and the way that notes should blend into each other (for example, are the notes smoothly bridged together or abruptly disconnected).

At first, work in small fragments. Incrementally, piece the small fragments you master together. Try to figure out where the musical phrases begin and end and point to the breaths where appropriate. As you move through the fragments, point out difficult passages and highlight them so that you can go back later and study them separately.

Next, try stringing together the different fragments of the piece you have studied. Play the song very slow at first, until you are able to play it from beginning to end. Then you can start increasing the speed little by little.

Once you are able to string together the different parts, polish the piece in terms of your breathing, rhythm, tuning, and performance. At this time, I highly recommend playing with a metronome. It will help you keep a better track of these aspects. Once you have mastered them after some time of practice, you will be able to play the song without it with confidence.

As you play, it is also helpful to think about the meaning, feeling, and historical setting of the piece. This will help transport you to its origin and let you deliver a more genuine interpretation of the song. For technical precision, you can also try practicing the scales and arpeggios related to the tonality of the work in addition to the music piece itself.

Finally, don't kickstart the study of a certain musical piece with a two-hour practice session the first day and then put off your next session forever. Remember that consistency is the most effective and will always yield the best results. Remain committed to your practice with frequent study sessions until you are able to reach the objective.

The techniques above are ideal for the study of a musical piece, but how should you approach a different kind of activity during practice sessions? The study of the saxophone technique or methodology requires a slightly different approach. If you are going to be completing exercises, preferably choose a set of technical exercises that will help you with a certain learning objective. Focus each session to a single objective so that you can better concentrate on your goals.

The overall distribution of time for your study sessions and study plan will depend one hundred percent on the specific objectives you set for yourself and your current level. Yet, I suggest the following distribution of practice time, as it is generally what I stick to in my own saxophone classes and my personal study:

- Technical practice, which includes scales, the study of musical language, breathing improvement, and other exercises should make up about 40% of the total time you spend practicing in a month. During this time, you can work on improving and learning the notes, scales, and musical scores. You can also learn more about note articulation, sound emission, and tuning.

- You can attribute the remaining 60% of the time to studying musical works and songs, which allow you to put the technical knowledge you are acquiring into practice. I generally recommend spending more time on musical pieces because, generally speaking, it is the aspect of music that most interests the beginner student. After all, the point of playing an instrument is to be able to perform different songs by using it.

Saxophone Finger Placement

The index, middle, and ring fingers of the left hand should cover the upper palm keys of the instrument, placing the finger in a natural order. Your right-hand fingers will be used to cover the lower set of palm keys, while the thumb is placed under the lower hook to support the weight of the instrument. Not all the weight of the instrument relies on the thumb since the neck strap of the instrument also actively provides support.

When the fingers are placed on the keys, you must be especially careful to keep them in their rightful place and avoid trespassing into other designated areas. As you position each finger, using the right pressure is also important. As you gain experience in your saxophone practice, you will learn to master the use of your fingers, pressing with them in a way that is firm yet soft, allowing them to flow with flexibility over the instrument. You should take care not to lift your finger too much as you play and to keep them in an arched position.

Learning The Saxophone's Notes

Just like you should learn how to hold your sax, you should also become familiar with the different musical notes you can play and how to locate them in the saxophone. Each note of the sax is made up of open and closed keys; these are activated by pressing each of the instrument's buttons. To be able to play any musical piece, it is important that you study and memorize each key box so that as you read any sheet of music, you can know which button to press. The note C, for example, can be played by pressing on the large button found on top of the saxophone.

At this point, it is also important that you start learning more about the musical language so that you can master the skill of reading notes on sheet music. This is very important for your musical learning journey, not only for the saxophone but for nearly any other instrument. Each score is made up of five lines, which together are known as a stave. Each score has a record in the form of the treble clef or A, in addition to showing each measure per minute of a song.

The notes you see on the highest to the lowest lines go in this order; F, D, G, B, and E. Each note in the line spacing in the lowest registers on the staff and ordered from highest to lowest are E, C, D, and F.

At first, memorizing all of these terms can seem overwhelming, but over time and with enough practice, reading musical notes can become as natural as reading in a second language. If you are really struggling, taking a music class can help. Nonetheless, there are many helpful resources online, available for free, that can help. However, some people perform better when they have the support of a teacher or fellow students.

Practice Exercises for Memorizing Notes on the Saxophone
The first note to practice is the first note you can play on the saxophone when following the order of the keys, C sharp. The reason

why we start with C Sharp and not the natural C is that the natural C requires you to press on the saxophone's keys. On the other hand, C sharp is played by simply blowing air into the instrument. That is when you don't press any keys and leave your playing fingers at rest, except for your thumbs.

The simplicity involved in playing this note makes it a great exercise for beginners. Practicing playing this note is highly recommended for playing practice as you are just getting started. Once you have played this note a few times, practice holding the sound for a longer time, this exercise will help you gain initial confidence and security in your ability for sound emission and will help you move forward as you try more complex notes and exercises. As a beginner, try practicing the C sharp note on a daily basis, for at least 5 minutes a day and try to hold onto the note on some of the notes.

The second of the notes on the saxophone, C, is the next note you should start practicing. The C note is obviously going to be very important since you will find it present in an abundance of simple and complex pieces. The C note is also the note on which the scale begins and is considered the central note of the saxophone. That means that you will find exactly the same number of notes above and below the C note. To play a natural C, use your left hand and place your middle finger over the middle or central key of your saxophone. Practice playing this note several times, and like with the previous exercise, try holding the sound for longer periods of time.

Going in descending order, the next note you will focus on practicing is the B note. This ordered approach, covering one note at a time, will make your practice more manageable, especially since it allows you to start with notes that have simple fingering. Playing this note requires only one finger, your index fingered, placed on the next note up, above the central note or the natural C, which was mentioned previously.

Next, you should practice the letter A. To play the note we will use two fingers, the index and the middle of the left hand. The left thumb is always resting in place, just below the octave key. As we learn different notes, it is good that we change the notes to compare their different sounds.

As you progress, you can move to more complex notes that involve the use of several fingers. The next note you should practice with is G. This note requires that we use three fingers because we are now closing three keys. At first, the note may not sound good, or may not sound at all. But that does not have to worry us. We need practice and time for the sound to come out right. The more keys we have to close, the greater difficulty we will have to emit the sound. So we start with notes that are easier to play.

All of the notes mentioned above have been played using the left hand and the upper set of three keys. Once you feel confident playing these first three notes and are able to emit sound properly, you can start practicing notes that use the right hand and require more complex finger placement. It is important that you first focus on gaining confidence in the first three notes, focusing on your breathing and the fullness of sound. It is always best to master simple skills fully before moving on without a strong knowledge base.

Notes D, E, and F are the next notes you should practice. All of these notes will require the use of your right-hand fingers, closing the lower set of three keys. To get started, you should follow descending order according to finger placement, and start learning note F. To play this note, all three keys on the left hand should be closed. Additionally, you will have to close the first note, located at the top of the lower set of keys, using your right-hand index finger. This will be the first note you'll practice using both of your hands and over three fingers.

After you have practiced the F note, you can move on with the next note in descending order, note E. As with the previous note, all three left-handed keys should be closed, using the index, middle, and ring fingers respectively. On the right hand, the first key should be closed with the index finger, and the second key should be closed using the middle finger. Finally, to play note E, you must close the three upper-level keys using your left hand and the three low keys using the right hand. When you play E, both of your hands will be fully engaged, with three fingers on each of your hands closing down on their respective keys.

Stringing Notes Together

Once you have a few notes under your belt, you can start practicing stringing notes together. The best way to approach this is, like with the note learning approach, to take small baby steps. Work in descending order and start trying to string the first two notes together. Once you can string the first two notes, then add a third one and so on.

Keep practicing the notes you learned until you are able to do an exercise connecting all of them. This type of exercise is called a scale. As a helpful tip, remember that practicing scales in descending order, that is, from the C note to the G note, is easier and tends to feel more natural. This is because by closing the keys progressively, the instrument will maintain the sound. Starting with low sounds is more difficult than starting with high sounds.

I suggest you start practicing the C scale first. To do this, you need to play the following notes: C - D - E - F - G - A – B. Work from C to B and then work your way back up in the opposite order. Next, you can move on to practice the D scale and its corresponding notes, which are: D - E - F# - G - A - B - C#. Again play the song in the order listed and then go back up the scale in the opposite order. Next, you can practice the E scale, which includes the following notes: E - F# - G# - A - B - C# - D#. In this way, you can continue working through the remaining scales, including the F, G, A, and B scales.

If at first, you find this exercise challenging, don't get discouraged. Play strings of two or three notes before working up to a full scale. Regardless of what stage you are at, don't ignore the importance of practice. Daily practice of your scales is the key to improvement, even if at first you find it challenging or the sound isn't perfect. Over time you will grow confident in sound emission and also memorize the notes on the instrument.

Sound Emission

Clean and robust sound emission is very important for the saxophone player. Being able to produce clear sounding notes that are strong and enunciated is key for the musician. There are several small tips and changes you can apply to improve your sound emission, even as a beginner.

When you are playing, try to keep the lips bent over the teeth. This will help you avoid making contact on the mouthpiece and the reed with your teeth. Depending on the shape of your mouth and what you are most comfortable with, you can choose to place the reed resting on the upper or lower lip.

For best results, allow the mouthpiece to enter your mouth up to the third or fourth line of the clamp. Keep your lips engaged, in order to put a light pressure over the mouthpiece with them. Use the lip that corresponds to the reed to provide support, preferably on the thickest part of the reed. This force used for support should be of considerable strength depending on how high or low the sound you are looking to produce is. For sounds that aren't particularly high or low, but that fall in the middle of the spectrum, the lip pressure you use to support the reed should be moderate or feel natural. To produce high pitched sounds, on the other hand, try using more strength to press down on the mouthpiece. As you do this, fold your lips more intently over your teeth and allow the mouthpiece to enter your mouth cavity a little more as the sound escapes the instrument. Finally, for low pitched sound, try gradually loosening the mouthpiece as you play. As the sound lowers and deepens, progressively loosen your grip.

To improve the emission and equality of sound, we recommend you support the flat part of the reed that remains inside the mouth after the lips have been bent over your teeth. You can verify sound by bringing the tip of your tongue closer to the tip of the mouthpiece and then quickly withdraw it at the same time. This will help you give the air a greater impulse and allow you to direct it through the opening formed between the mouthpiece and the reed. The movement of the tongue has to be fast, as mentioned before. Move your tongue as if you were quickly trying to spit out any little object from your mouth.

Sound modulations are just as important to improve our overall sound emission. When emitting the sound with the mouthpiece, we have to modulate it through different small actions. First, we must adjust the pressure that the upper and lower jaw exerts on the instrument. This pressure should not be too strong because, with excessive strength, the reed would be constricted and, therefore, would not be able to vibrate. As a result, the increased pressure will prevent the reed from producing sound. At the same time, avoid loosening up the pressure too much. When the reed is too loose, air won't be properly directed to pass through the reed, preventing the proper formation of the air column.

At this stage, you must choose a reed that is not too challenging to use to start with. As a beginner, the wrong kind of reed will pose excessive difficulty and prevent you from properly emitting sound. A 1 or 1 and a half reed or even up to a number 2 reed should perfectly suffice. If you aren't certain, you can ask at the music store about their reed availability and their recommendations. Pay close attention to the strength you use during the contraction of your lips. You should also control the pressure used to blow air out and into the instrument. This should be done from the bottom, using the muscle of the diaphragm. Keeping all of these recommendations in mind during your daily practice will help you make some evident progress in the quality of your sound emission. At first, it might require great concentration and conscious effort to apply these small changes. However, the more you practice, the more accustomed you will become to these techniques, and eventually, they will become second nature to you.

The Mouth and Sound Emission

The position of the throat and the oral cavity when playing the saxophone are aspects of great relevance for the production of sound. They are closely related to the saxophone's mouthpiece. This is because the throat generates different movements and vibrations when you are playing each unique note. This means that there are specific points of movement the throat and mouth will make to emulate each note. In fact, millimetric movement changes of the throat, tongue, and lips are required to differentiate one note from another one.

The foundation that supports this movement must have very good support; said the foundation is air, element which must always be exhaled using uniform pressure, pushed outward by the diaphragm muscle. This way, it can enter in a firm and immutable form into the mouthpiece.

When the air is constant and the movement in the throat and the oral cavity act in balance, a stable sound is produced that does not break and simply flows towards a set point. That is a current of air that has a direction and intention. The said concept must be internalized from the mouthpiece to be applied later in the saxophone performance. Once made it should be appreciated that the movement of the imposition made to produce notes is much less than that made with the mouthpiece, offering the possibility of making much longer interval jumps at high speeds since the air is stable and continuous.

The mouthpiece allows the interpreter to understand that the imposition is necessary when executing register changes on the saxophone and that the distance between each note is minimal, the same as that required when singing, the mouthpiece being a means to make visible the problems of records link. To propose the development of this concept, work without an instrument must be carried out in the first instance to understand that the relationship evoked between the song and the notes of the mouthpiece. This gives the interpreter awareness in the domain of movement that is generated in the throat. These movements are the same when singing and playing the mouthpiece, and the development of the mouthpiece and its relationship with other resources such as attacks or registration will revolve around them.

Learning To Breathe For The Saxophone

The saxophone is a wind instrument, which means that your breathing is not only an important element but essential to playing any musical piece. The better you become at controlling your breathing, the better the saxophone player you will become.

In very simple terms, breathing is nothing more than the physiological process by which human beings take in air and with it oxygen, and then after the gas exchange has occurred, expel air releasing with it carbon dioxide. However, when it comes to playing a wind instrument, we must stop thinking about breathing as a mindless instinctive action and start becoming more conscious about how we breathe. Controlled breathing is undoubtedly the result of good training and can help you improve greatly in your practice.

In this section of the book, we will concentrate on breathing, but more specifically, on the many ways in which you can breathe to benefit your saxophone playing. We'll learn about how saxophonists place their lips, jaws, mouth, or nose at the moment of controlling the air while playing. When you play a wind instrument, you must learn how to breathe quickly while being able to fill your lungs with air completely. This can be mastered with the help of some very basic breathing exercises that can be built up progressively as you advance in your training.

Each player has their own method to control their breathing. Some breathe through the corner of their lips; others breathe by opening their mouth and dropping the lower jaw, others breathe by opening the upper jaw without moving the lower jaw, while others breathe through their nose.

Breathing Through Lip Corners

This type of breathing is typically fast and deep. To master it, you must practice breathing without moving the mouth, only opening the lips sideways, as if you wanted the corners of your lips to rise and to touch your ears with them as you breathe. With this type of breathing, the mouthpiece of the saxophone does not move because it helps with the orbicular and other muscles which remain strong.

This type of mouthpiece support and breathing is typically used to obtain a sweet, warm, and very classic sound that is ideal for the sound of an orchestra. One benefit you can experience by breathing through lip corners is that it allows you to have greater control over the air you exhale and allows you to do so with greater pressure. However, some experts criticize this breathing style because they say that when air exits through the corners of the lips, it produces additional noise. Some also claim that, with this method of breathing, it takes more time to get in a deep breath.

Breathing Through The Mouth With A Lower Jaw

This type of breathing is not very common in classical saxophone. This breathing style involves breathing by modifying the position of your lower lip on the reed a little. Then, when the time comes to inhale, you let your jaw drop to allow air to enter and then immediately raise the jaw, placing it straight back into its original position over the mouthpiece. This breathing style can be seen the most among some renowned Jazz saxophonists. They claim to prefer this breathing method because they consider that this form of breathing is deeper and faster.

As an additional benefit, this movement of the lower jaw allows the player to practice the study of vibrato, which is widely used in the genre. However, just like it has some strengths, this breathing style also has some disadvantages. Some cons of this breathing style are that the column of exhaled air is less full and more unstable, which translates into less security for the precise emission of sound when targeting a note.

Breathing Focused On The Upper Jaw

While some saxophone players vouch for controlling air with the lower jaw, others oppose this view. Opposers claim that the lower jaw and lip should be in direct contact with the reed and should therefore not be moved during breathing. For this reason, other jazz sax players prefer to breathe by elevating the upper lip, since this upper part of the mouth is only in direct contact with the mouthpiece. By not interacting with the reed, this type of breathing is less likely to affect the quality of sound.

Breathing Through The Nose

When we are not playing and simply going through our regular daily activities, we normally breathe through the nose. Yet when we are playing a wind instrument, we hardly have time to breathe through the nose. Most commonly, you will find that players adapt their breathing in some of the ways that I have previously mentioned, mainly through the corner of the lips. Some of the downsides of breathing through the nose are that it is slower and doesn't allow us to get a deep enough inhalation. Is a saxophone player were to attempt to use nasal breathing when playing, they'd find themselves quickly fatigued. As an exemption, there's a group of saxophonist supporters of nasal breathing who have managed to incorporate it in their technique. However, they don't depend entirely on nasal breathing. Instead, they combine nasal and mouth breathing in a circular pattern. As you are just starting out, the most important thing to remember is that nasal breathing, on its own, is not a good choice for the saxophone.

Which Breathing Style Is The Best?

How can you determine which breathing style is best, or more precisely, which one will help you achieve the best results in your saxophone journey? To figure out the answer, you must not forget that all these different ways of breathing are closely related to the diverse types of jaws that each saxophonist has. Some jaw types include squared, salient, or withdrawn. Any of these breathing styles mentioned above are in close relation with these morphological features. Therefore as a new player, the very first thing you must do is take a deep look at your own physical characteristics and determine which breathing style adapts best to your body.

You must practice the most appropriate respiratory technique according to your own anatomy and physiology. Overall, you should use any method or breathing exercise that will lead to faster and deeper breathing. This deep fast breathing will allow you to achieve a fluid and constant exhalation of air that forms the strong and robust air column that's ideal for playing.

Air must be exhaled slowly but strongly from our lungs. All the while, you must take special care to avoid inflating your cheeks. A good tip you should try is observing some saxophonists play in recorded performances. Pay attention to their breathing as they play and compare saxophone players of different genres, such as classical and jazz, and draw your own conclusions. You'll soon notice that some musicians also, in their usual playing styles, combine several of these breathing methods. To be able to play effortlessly, you must find a way to breathe that makes your face and movements as elegant and firm as possible.

Practice- Simple Breathing Exercise

This first exercise we will be going over is focused on improving concentration, resistance, and air control. To complete this exercise, you must exhale air through the nose with a strong dry blow. The diaphragm muscle must support this movement. Next, you must inhale air back in again. The inhalation must be as strong as the exhalation. However, you must be wary of avoiding any contractions of the throat. These are evidenced by the production of forced or guttural sounds, which shouldn't occur. This exercise is completed in fixed pulses, without any long pauses. At first, this might be challenging, but it will help you increase your air control over time.

To start with, try four series of ten exhalations and inhalations. These should be made over a period of one minute, followed by a short rest period. This exercise will help you learn to inhale more abundant amounts of air quickly. At this stage, we would be practicing breathing as a natural act. This concept must be carried out into technical exercises at first, working only with the mouthpiece and then executed on the saxophone. Throughout all of this, bear in mind that the lips should not ever separate from the mouthpiece. At the same time, you should allow the left and right ends of the lips to open up for a deeper breathe.

Practice: Breathing Exercise To Develop Air Control

Next, you can practice this next exercise, which mainly focuses on developing better control of the air column. Taking only the mouthpiece, place the thumb, either left or right, at the bottom of the mouthpiece, at the base where the reed would be placed.

With the mouthpiece and your lips in the position described above, try breathing deeply as if you were yawning. As you do this, avoid lifting your shoulders at the same time. Open the left and right part of the mouth but firmly grip the lower and upper lip all at once. As you do this, the air taken in freely enters the body, first filling the lower abdomen, then the diaphragm and ribs, finally the high chest and up to the clavicle. If, in the process of taking air, you hear a forced sound, you must pause and repeat the exercise one more time. Here, the important thing is to learn to take in air without generating tension. As a result, you will be able to breathe in larger amounts of air naturally and comfortably. You don't have to keep a specific breathing pace or speed. Feel free to complete these breathing exercises at your own pace.

After breathing in and holding air in for a few moments, the air should be exhaled through the mouthpiece naturally. This is achieved with the support of the diaphragm, which participates in the exhalation of the air. Completing this using the mouthpiece will help you better understand how breathing works when you are really playing the saxophone. Notice that the air is released normally and that exhalation should continue until there are no air residues in your lungs. Identifying the moment when you run out of the air is very important. Once you reach this point, it is recommended that you hold on a few seconds before going through the exercise again. Determine when you are ready to start again and repeat the exercise.

Practice: Breathing Exercise To Build Resistance And Boost Breathing Capacity

Next, we are going to practice a breathing exercise that will help you increase your breathing capacity, which is an important goal for every saxophonist, beginner, or advanced. Start by taking in air as it has been described in the previous breathing exercises. As you hold air in, place the thumb in your right hand inside your mouth, so that it is occupying the space that the mouthpiece and reed should take up. Next, try exhaling the entire volume of air held within your lungs as fast as possible. After doing so, you should feel like your chest is completely vacant.

After that first breathing cycling, you will complete a second one. Again, take in the air very quickly, but this time exhale it in a relaxed fashion. This entire two breathing cycle process should be completed, at first, about fifteen times per series for a total of three series.

The way you should complete these exercises is by not going through all the three series at once. Instead, you should insert these breathing series between other technical saxophone exercises you perform during a regular practice session. As you become better at performing this breathing exercise, you can start increasing the number of breaths within each series and then increase the number of series to complete themselves.

Chapter 4

Saxophone Care and Maintenance

This book was created to pro0vide the saxophone beginner with as much useful and valuable information as possible. For this reason, I have decided to continue with a subject of great importance, but one that saxophone teachers often neglect or forget to talk about. Learning about the cleaning and maintenance routine of the saxophone should be as important for any musician as the act of learning to play the notes themselves.

Instrument maintenance is not a minor issue. The correct operation and performance of the instrument, just as the length of the saxophone's useful life, depends entirely on how much care the instrument receives and how well it is handled, carried, and stored.

I have come across students who, despite being months into their saxophone learning journey, have never stopped once to think about this subject. For many, this has caused them subsequent inconveniences that have affected their instrument's integrity, sound emission, and function.

As I mentioned before, having an instrument that is in good condition is vital for obtaining good results. You could be an excellent saxophone player, but if your instrument becomes damaged or dysfunctional, notes and sounds will be off despite your best techniques. There is no doubt that the care you give your instrument is vital for your saxophone to work well and do its job.

Now, there are instruments that, thanks to their excellent manufacturing and high-quality materials, are a little more resistant and, therefore, more durable. But others aren't made with such a high degree of resistance. This is often true of most beginner saxophones since many choose cheaper or even used instruments when they are just starting out. These kinds of saxophones will require a lot more effort from your part. You will have to make sure to offer them the proper care to avoid experiencing any setbacks in your practice. Fortunately, the care of your sax is not very complicated. The most important thing where maintenance is concerned is that you are focused and committed to acquiring good habits to protect it.

Novice players often overlook saxophone maintenance. Unfortunately, most saxophone newbies only realize how important having a proper cleaning and maintenance routine when their instrument shows signs of wear and tear. The longevity and performance of your instrument are highly dependent on the care you give it. The earlier you start paying attention to proper care recommendations, the better your instrument will work. As a result, you can better prevent damage and avoid having to lose out on practice time during lengthy or even costly repair work. It doesn't matter if you are a professional or just in your first month of classes. You must always take into account the cleaning and maintenance guidelines to have an optimal function and durability of your Saxophone.

A saxophone maintenance routine doesn't have to be overly time consuming or complex. You can get started by following very basic steps. The small actions mentioned below can help you lengthen the life of your instrument and keep its sound true and beautiful.

Keep Sugar Away From The Sax

While taking care of your saxophone as you practice is very important, most fail to realize that what we do before and after we play our instrument also matters. As a wind instrument, the mouth plays a leading role in the mastery of the instrument. As a result, anything going on inside your mouth can directly affect the sound of your saxophone. To the surprise of many, even food and liquid residue can have a negative effect on your saxophone.

To avoid any unnecessary problems, avoid drinking soda, juice, or any other liquid that contains sugar before playing the instrument. Since you will be placing the mouthpiece directly into your mound and blowing into the instrument to produce sound, sugars can travel into your instrument and accumulate in its inner components.

This is especially concerning because sugar is corrosive. If sugar manages to enter the saxophone, it can easily stick to smaller inner parts and even crystalize inside the instrument. As a result, the metal and keys can suffer some major deterioration. In case your instrument was to be severely damaged, the repairs can turn out to be very expensive.

The most important takeaway from this information is the importance of mouth rinsing and teeth washing before playing the saxophone though it might seem like a tedious and unnecessary precaution to take; at the end of the day, it could end up saving you a lot of trouble and several dollars.

Care of the Cork

It is very important to apply cork grease to the cork of the pipe before assembling the mouthpiece and to, at all costs, avoid storing the saxophone with the mouthpiece mounted on the neck. These two actions will lengthen the life of the cork and will avoid future wear or damage.

During the first few weeks of working with a new instrument, taking the time to grease the cork on a frequent basis, and properly, will be essential. As time passes and you have given your instrument more use, you will notice that cork grease applications can be more spaced out in time. Nevertheless, remember that you should never use force when assembling the pieces of a saxophone. If you force the cork, it will most likely break off, and you will have to repair it. Most likely, even with the right materials and tools, you won't be able to fix this on your own and will have to visit a professional. For its correct assembly, it is necessary to fit the cork into the neck using little turning movements. While doing so, be careful not to apply excessive force on the octave key.

Keep Your Instrument Dry

When you finish playing your instrument, it is likely that the instrument will be humid or will have collected moisture to a certain degree. This is due to the very nature of the instrument. For one, the mouthpiece houses a reed that is humidified with saliva before playing. At the same time, the instrument's mouthpiece is positioned within the mouth and played through the flow of air. Since air is exhaled through the mouth, saliva particles can easily travel into the instrument.

You should by no means ever put down your instrument and store it in this condition. After playing, you should always take time to dry your saxophone thoroughly. To dry the sax, take a smooth rag and attach it to a counterbalanced rope. Then pass the rag directly through the neck or the part between the mouthpiece and the body of the instrument.

Repeat the same process with the body of the saxophone. First, tuck the rope through the top of the body and pull it out through the hood, so that the rag can brush the inside and remove moisture from this area as it passes through.

For the safety of your instrument, we do not recommend ever using a brush to dry or clean your saxophone. While a brush should generally not be used on any surface of the saxophone, it is especially important to highlight that a brush can cause severe damage if it is inserted into the body of the instrument, so this should be avoided at all costs. Ignoring this recommendation will inevitably result in the shortening of the saxophone's lifespan.

To further reduce moisture within the instrument, you should take some basic precautions before storing it away. For best results, after you place the saxophone inside its case, we recommend leaving the case open for about five to ten minutes if possible. This will allow any moisture that remains inside the instrument to evaporate before the case is closed. Otherwise, the humidity will remain trapped inside the saxophone case.

Clean the Mouthpiece

The mouthpiece, as its name implies, is in direct contact with the oral cavity and everything this contains. This includes food residue, saliva, and a wide variety of bacteria. This is why it is important to pay special attention to the hygiene of this particular piece during your cleaning routine.

Try to clean the mouthpiece using warm water regularly and, if strictly necessary, a small amount of neutral soap. However, you should never use other types of detergents, especially harsh ones like bleach. If you are using a gentle soap, apply it to the mouthpiece using a small brush with soft bristles that can easily pass through the opening of the mouthpiece to clean the inside surface. After you have completely cleaned the surface using a gentle soap and a brush, completely rinse out the mouthpiece. If necessary, give an additional rinse to confirm no soap residue remains. Finally, dry both the external and internal surface of the mouthpiece using kitchen paper or another similar type of soft paper that won't leave signs of small debris. Once the mouthpiece is dry, you can safely place it back into the saxophone's case for storage.

Remember that this is the one part of the saxophone that is in the most direct contact with your mouth, so its hygiene is crucial.

Get Your Instrument Professionally Checked-Out

If you enjoy learning to play the saxophone and being able to practice regularly, giving it proper maintenance is essential to maintain its functionality. Taking the instrument to be periodically evaluated by a professional every 12-18 months is an easy way to prevent major issues and minimize lost time involved in repairs or trouble-shooting.

With regular use, your instrument can start to show signs of wear or require some minor adjustments. These small issues or alterations, when ignored, can not only affect your instrument physically, but it can also impair your musical learning process. Sound modifications or function differences in your instrument can easily go unnoticed. As you continue to practice using an instrument that is not in decent shape, you will subconsciously start making adjustments to compensate for the alterations. Eventually, but especially as a beginner, can lead to the development of bad habits in technique. Later on, getting rid of these bad habits and learning to play according to best practices can become even more challenging.

Cleaning Your Saxophone

Taking care of yourself involves a regular hygiene routine. In the same way, all the objects we consider valuable in our daily lives, from our cars to our clothing garments require frequent cleaning for proper maintenance. Likewise, our saxophones must be properly cleaned to avoid unnecessary damage and wear.

Maintaining a clean, damage-free instrument depends not only on the actual cleaning routine you follow for your instrument. The way you handle your instrument, the posture you maintain while playing, whether you play with food or liquid residue in your mouth, and other factors also play an important role in the maintenance of an instrument.

In this section of the book, we are going to focus on the basic hygiene principles for the saxophone, which, as we know, is a wind instrument. It is important to constantly factor in the fact that the saxophone is a wind instrument because it will help us identify common sources of bacteria and other contamination. A good hygiene routine will consider all the parts, both external and internal.

The saxophone player relies on two main tools to produce sound and music - the fingers, which press on keys, and the mouth, which is used to produce an air current causing sound vibrations. Since our hands and our mouths are constantly in contact with the instrument, these must be the first aspects addressed during a basic cleaning regime.

Daily Hygiene

Some very basic cleaning tasks should be performed daily for the proper maintenance of your saxophone. Among them, one of the most important ones is drying off humidity from all the different instrument parts. As we have mentioned before, humidity is one of the saxophone's greatest enemies and can cause damage both to the inner and outer surfaces of the instrument. For this reason, the saxophone must be entirely dried off using the appropriate cleaning cloths. You should also individually dry off each of the note keys that cover the small holes down the body of the instrument. This is preferably done with special absorbent paper, as this can prevent fungal growth in these areas. Yet, when you don't have absorbent paper available, you should still try to remove moisture from the keys to the best of your ability using some kind of gentle cloth or rag.

External cleaning of the saxophone is also a relevant chore to complete after each use of the instrument. This is especially important due to the metallic nature of the instrument. The saxophone is widely known due to its sleek, elegant, and shiny appearance. However, the glow of a saxophone is not maintained on its own. To keep your sax looking its best and to preserve its outward shine, you'll have to clean its external surface regularly. You can do this with a specialized microfiber cloth that is designed for the cleaning of this type of musical instrument. Selecting the right cloth will help you best protect the lacquer of the instrument. If your saxophone is silver, you'll need to select a specific cloth for this finish as well. The cloth should then be used all over the outer surface of the instrument to wipe down any sweat residue, moisture, dust, or any other sign of soiling.

As you grow in your skill and find yourself frequently performing on the saxophone, you might want to consider investing in more visually attractive cleaning cloths for your instrument. Special concert handkerchiefs or cloths are the best options for external cleaning in between and during performances with an audience. They are often modest and elegant and can be easily placed nearby while you play without looking tacky or drawing unnecessary attention. These cloths are typically also made out of microfiber or even silk.

Internal hygiene is as important if not more important than external hygiene. Therefore the inside of your saxophone should be cleaned regularly, preferably daily or after each use. There's no greater risk for a saxophone than accumulated moisture on the inner mechanics of the instrument. A daily cleaning routine is the best way to combat this problem, especially if you are practicing daily. Purchase a cloth that is well suited for the cleaning of the saxophone's inside. Try to select a cloth of good quality so that it protects your instrument better and lasts you for a longer time. Using the wrong cloth or cleaning material could put the safety of your instrument at risk and even cause internal scratches. The size of the cloth is also important since a too large cloth can easily become stuck inside the neck or body of the saxophone. A good source for your cleaning materials is specialized Saxophone stores, which often carry special cloths designed for this purpose. You can even find specific clothes and rag models that are tailored for Alto, Tenor, Soprano or Baritone saxophone varieties.

You should always carry clean rags with you to be fully prepared. For the best results, I recommend storing your dry rags in different compartments, separate from used rags. The cleaning cloths that have already been used to wipe down the inside and outside of the instrument or to dry your mouthpiece will absorb humidity in the process. Therefore if they are stored next to dry drags, some moisture can transfer to the clean textiles. Additionally, I recommend keeping the used drags out of the case for a while after they've been used. This will allow them to dry off as much as possible before they are stored in a closed space. Most importantly, you can prevent moisture from the rags by spreading them within your closed case to prevent odors from developing.

Once you have gone through these parts of your daily saxophone cleaning routine, working on the inside and outside, you should finish off cleaning the mouthpiece. Keeping a mouthpiece clean is essential, not just for aesthetics or longevity of the instrument, but for your own health and hygiene. We have already covered above how you should tackle the task of cleaning your mouthpiece. If preferred, you can also purchase special sprays that are used as mouthpiece cleaners to complement the process.

While it might seem like maintenance overkill, it is also necessary to take proper care of the saxophone's case to preserve the hygiene and integrity of your instrument. After you've completed your daily post-practice or post-performance maintenance, you should also take a few actions to take care of the saxophone's home. If the saxophone is clean and cared for completely, on both the inner and outer surfaces, but its sleeve or case is not, the work invested in the cleaning of the instrument may very well be in vain.

Smells can easily occur within an instrument and its case, especially so when cleaning isn't thorough. These smells, when not removed or neutralized, can begin to impregnate the surfaces and become permanent features of your instrument and case. For this reason, we recommend using a special saxophone case deodorants.

Different options on the market range from the aromatic to solutions with a biological and antibacterial function. Deodorants, when combined with good saxophone case ventilation, are the best approach to eliminating and preventing moisture and the start of odors. A good tip to increase instrument and case ventilation and reduce humidity, which is a common cause for bad smells, is to develop the habit of not closing the case immediately after the saxophone is stored. Allowing the case to remain open prevents odors from being sealed in.

When storing the saxophone in its case, it is important to consider that the neck and mouthpiece must be kept separately. Each of these saxophone parts should be individually wrapped in a piece of cloth of appropriate material and consistency. The cloth should be of a size that is large enough to fit each piece in, but also small enough so that it can be easily sorted within the proper accessory compartment.

If you weren't already regularly brushing your teeth for your own health and hygiene, picking up the saxophone might motivate you to do so. Oral-dental hygiene is extremely important for proper saxophone maintenance. For best results, you must avoid consuming any taking sugary drinks or any type of solid food immediately before a saxophone study session or performance. As mentioned above, the residual sugars in exhaled air can travel down into the instrument and cling to the surface as residue, which can lead to serious problems. If you do happen to eat or drink something immediately before a saxophone class or performance, be cautious enough to brush your teeth before playing the instrument.

Every day, you should also take general precautions regarding the general way in which you handle your saxophone. During your practice breaks or rest periods, do not leave the saxophone in its case, sleeve, on a chair, or any other random surface. If you are not yet ready to put your instrument away and call it a day, you should be using suitable support to hold it in place. This is the best choice to prevent any accidental damage and to avoid the spread of humidity within the many small parts of the saxophone and its case.

Cleaning and maintenance routines can be tedious, but improved care can lengthen the useful life of the instrument. It can also better maintain its sonic properties, making these extra steps and investing additional time after each session very worthwhile. We certainly recommend that you apply these helpful tips to your daily saxophone care ritual.

Weekly Hygiene

There are many microorganisms which grow and that you do not see, that love to live within humidity. This is the reason why, every week, you should be washing all of your used cleaning rags. It is recommended to wash all rags with hot water, at around 140 degrees

Fahrenheit, in a washing machine. Afterward, you must allow the cloths to dry well before storing them.

Every week or two weeks, you can also go ahead and grease corks. You must use the appropriate products, according to the recommendations of the instrument manufacturer. This will guarantee that the greasing products won't go inside your saxophone and accumulate within.

Monthly Hygiene

The cleaning, washing, and disinfecting of the saxophone's mouthpiece should be done roughly once a month, though it can be done sooner if you notice visible soiling or a bad smell. I highly recommend using spraying alcohol or other product with disinfection capabilities during this process. I do want to clarify that boiling water is not an acceptable method for mouthpiece disinfection. Attempting to boil your mouthpiece for its antibacterial properties will most likely result in damage to your mouthpiece. To wash the mouthpiece, simply use a mixture of gentle soap and water, applied with a small brush as mentioned before, and then rinse with abundant water.

Every month you should also complete reed cleaning. You can clean the reeds on your instrument by immersing them in a pot with hydrogen peroxide for a few seconds and rinsing them out.

Finally, every ten months to a year, take your saxophone into a professional for a general checkup. A professional will be able to properly evaluate your instrument and be able to determine whether any additional maintenance is needed.

Chapter 5

Selecting Didactic Material
for Your Practice

Normally the use of specific saxophone methodology works is neglected due to their little appeal in comparison to the study of concert repertoires or the development of improvisation skills. To a certain extent, this is understandable, as it is not of much interest to the public to hear about scales, arpeggios, harmonic tone progressions, etc.

This type of musical exercise is typically played mechanically. However, this technical work also has a very high value in musical training. Thanks to methodology books, we can acquire the necessary tools to function as musicians, whether as causal or professional performers or even composers. Inside or outside an academy, a solid technical musical foundation can be obtained through the study of technical exercises.

If we start studying methodological and technical resources with dedication, we will even expand our musical repertoire and enrich our improvisation for a wide variety of genres, such as classical, jazz, or traditional music. After all, these resources usually include knowledge and technical practice that is essential to improving our musical interpretation. For this reason, technical methodology books and documents have been used throughout history in the formation of saxophonists and other musicians.

There are several types of practice-based study resources novice students can use to guide their first study sessions. One of the most popular study materials are manuals or guide-like musical methods. These often include a compilation of ordered exercises that progressively increase in difficulty. This type of resource is one hundred percent exercise based.

Secondly, there are study resources that are exercise-based but include other types of useful additional information. These typically analyze concepts practiced in the workbook's exercises and include other helpful tips and reflections.

Finally, there are more ambitious saxophone practice books that attempt to impart knowledge by using musical pieces rather than simple exercises for practice. Typically this type of method, when geared to beginners, includes very simple songs. Nonetheless, those who are just starting out typically feel more comfortable exploring notes and exercises that can be strung together before attempting to play a full song. The main challenge with methods that are based on musical pieces is that other concerns such as timing and rhythm, which are often big elements in songs, can distract the beginner student from mastering the more elemental concepts.

Keep in mind that following a specific methodology presented in a technical resource is not an absolute requirement. Yet, it is extremely useful for some students since it provides an ordered source of exercise for daily practice. The student can then move through the content at their own pace and progressively work up to more difficult exercises on their own. Written information in these resource books can be studied over and over again and is always available for review. This is especially helpful for those that are looking to master the art of playing the saxophone without the guidance of an instructor due to time and financial constraints or personal preference.

However, you must not overlook the fact that a method or practice-based resource book is simply an optional learning resource one can use and not an ultimate solution for tackling the complex task of mastering an instrument. A resource book will not be able to resolve all the doubts and challenges a student will face during their learning journey. Ideally, practice books or methods should be considered as additional learning resources to enrich the learning process, but should not be the main focus or single resource used throughout your learning. Playing music is a dynamic process that requires the use of knowledgeful resources like this book, musical exercise resources, and support from instructors, friends, or even video-lessons in order to achieve full mastery of the instrument.

If used properly, an exercise book can become a very valuable tool in saxophone training. We should also keep in mind that for many beginner players out there, investing in a group or private lessons poses a financial challenge that is impossible for some students. If you are a prospective musician in this situation, you shouldn't feel discouraged. Books like this, with a wide set of resourceful information, paired with methodology based practice books and regular study time can lead to great results. A good instructor can simplify the process, but should not be considered elementary in the mastery of the instrument, especially at a beginner stage.

Chapter 6

Saxophone Sound Effects

Playing the saxophone involves a lot more than blowing air into a mouthpiece and pressing down on keys. This instrument is highly emotional and can communicate a lot about the interpreter's feelings. The saxophonist relies on many different skills in order to give their music a unique feel and sound. Among the most important techniques used to turn simple notes into art are different sound effects that the player can use while playing a variety of pieces. We'll explore a few of them below and give you some general pointers on how to start practicing them.

Vibrato

Vibrato is an effect that is generated with the mouthpiece and reed. What you have to do is once you have the mouthpiece inside the mouth, make a small movement to generate oscillation in the sound. In the video effects for saxophone, you can see how to make the vibrato. You will hear a small example without vibrato and then one with vibrato to make it clearer what the effect is.

In the example without vibrato, the notes sound smooth, steady, and firm, and it is a fine sound, and some notes are long. In the second example, we take advantage of the long notes to generate the vibrato and thus give a better expression of the instrument.

If you pay attention to the sound, you will notice that expressively, the difference between example 1 and example 2 is significant. What you have to do is identify the points with long notes and then generate the vibrato. There are many tips for achieving a better vibratory effect. The secret is with the help of a metronome practicing long four-beat oscillations. Another tip is to tighten and loosen the lip when playing the instrument to generate that sound.

The Growl

The growl is an interesting sound effect that can be produced by blowing out air and, at the same time, tensing the throat muscles to produce a growl like sound. Some have compared this technique to a forceful exhalation you might take to remove debris from the saxophone's air with a column of air. The result is a deep growl that has a "rocker" feel.

The Bend

Note bending is produced when a note is played, and you quickly loosen the grip on the mouthpiece at the same time. This will cause the note to play correctly and then the tuning to drop. Once the tuning drops, you should reaffirm your mouthpiece grip, which will allow normal air exhalation pressure to be recovered quickly. As a result, the note is heard at its real frequency, then it loses its tune and finally recovers its tune again. Basically, it is a controlled variation in tune that happens in a very quick way.

The Slap

To create a "slapping" sound effect, the tongue is placed parallel to the reed obstructing the opening. The player then blows air out strongly while the tongue is removed and then returned to its initial position. This produces a very dry, somewhat hollow musical timbre. It is better to try this effect on notes that are lower on the register. Additionally, it should be performed with care since, in inexperienced hands, it can damage or even destroy your reed.

Chapter 7

Tuning Your Saxophone

The skill of properly tuning any musical instrument, specifically the saxophone, is a long and tedious process that can take many years to be fully developed and, in most cases, requires a certain degree of musical knowledge. As a novice player, especially during your first days of practice, attempting to tackle the tuning of your sax on your own is next to impossible. However, as you start familiarizing yourself with the instrument and its sound, it is certainly a task that can be successfully developed.

There are no great tricks or secret formulas you can follow to help you play in tune. Only work and perseverance will help you be able to recognize and replicate the ideal sounds of the instrument. The most important thing is that you become aware of different sounds that the saxophone produces so that you can later work to improve your playing using these sounds as a reference. The more you get used to playing, but most importantly, the more you get used to listening, the easier it will be for you to develop the necessary skills required for accurately tuning your instrument.

A good place to start tackling this skill is with the study of musical language, the cultivation of technical knowledge on the instrument, and the training of your musical ear to examine the characteristic saxophone sounds properly. You can follow up on your study by practicing using exercises designed to improve and control the pitch of sound with your instrument.

Overall, the most important asset you will have throughout this process is your sense of hearing. You should work as much as possible on improving your musical ear and sharpening your ability to recognize different notes and sounds on the saxophone. To get started, we will go over some basic information on training your musical ear to not only improve your beginner saxophone performance but also to help you become a better, well-rounded musician overall.

Educating Your Musical Ear

The greatest tool you can use to develop your musical ear is a hundred percent free and easy to work it. We are talking about your voice, more precisely your singing voice. While singing might seem completely unrelated to the art of playing the saxophone, it can be a powerful tool to use for developing your musical ear, which in turn will make you a better saxophone player. Additionally, singing starts by helping you develop your breathing muscles, which will also positively benefit you as a saxophonist.

Remember that it is not essential for you to become an outstanding singer. The point of practicing singing exercises is simply to contribute to the training of your musical ear and help you become a better musician overall. The practice of singing and the development of all parts of your voice production system, including the soft palate, tongue, and larynx, are an essential part of learning to listen and identify different musical sounds. At the same time, taking the time to learn a musical language is an important tool to help you master any melodic and harmonic musical system.

For anyone learning how to play a musical instrument, sound, above everything else, should be the main "concern" or the main element you examine when evaluating your performance. After all, technique, musical theory, and practice all focus on the education and growth of a musician who can play a song that is pleasant to the ear and enjoyed by an audience.

To be able to determine whether you are producing accurate and pleasant sounds when you are playing saxophone, you will need to be able to identify whether you are playing in tune or not. If you identify that you are playing out of tune, you can then work to make the necessary corrections.

We define correct tuning as the act of playing an instrument in a way that produces a sound that is as close as possible to the most accepted tone and sound system that is accepted. One of the most useful tuning devices available is, in fact, embedded in our bodies. Our powerful ears provide us with an acute hearing sense that allows us to recognize different sounds. Next, we will discuss how our hearing mechanisms contribute to helping us properly tune our instruments when playing.

Tuning Your Saxophone and The Inner Ear

Our inner ear is the sensor that constantly helps us determine whether a sound is harmonious and in perfect tune or is out of pitch and unpleasant to listen to. Our ears must know how well-tuned notes should sound so that our brains can correctly interpret sound vibrations based on those internal references and properly understand sounds.

When sound vibrations travel through the many small inner parts within the human ear, the sound will be directed to move down the canal and activate several sensory pathways that work to communicate auditory messages to the brain. The brain then interprets this message and accurately directs our entire bodies to react.

When interpreting musical pieces, the signals that our brain sends provides us with information and understanding about the quality of saxophone playing performance. We can use conclusions drawn from our interpretation of sound to guide our muscles, fingers, and breathing. By helping us determine whether correction of any aspect of our playing technique is required, our inner ear, when properly trained, can help us correct important tuning issues. As a result, we will be able to improve the quality of our sound transmission when we play. That flexibility, which is achieved with training, will be one of the key pieces in achieving your goal of becoming a successful saxophone player.

In my opinion, one of the biggest mistakes made when learning to tune an instrument, as a beginner to intermediate student, is mainly caused by the use of a tuner device. Using a tuner device must be done exclusively when the instrument player requires special insight to be able to conclude whether their instrument has a correct sound and whether that sound is considered well-tuned or out of tune.

Basically, the tuner, as a device, shouldn't be considered a full solution to a problem, but instead, be used as a convenient aid if the need for it arises. The information that a tuner can give us should serve as a general reference, being able to alert us about sound issues with the different notes played on our saxophones.

Yet, as useful and important as this device is, it can create some bad habits. In a way, when we are fully trusting our sound tuning to a tuner device, we are succumbing to laziness. Rather than working on developing the skills of our inner ear, we let the device do all the hard work. If, as beginners, we start using this device to figure out whether our sounds are too high or low, we won't ever be able to develop the necessary skills to figure this out on our own.

At the end of the day, if not used with caution, a tuner device can end up causing more harm than good. It can even keep you from developing the necessary skills to learn to recognize this sound imbalance through your own audition. This way, all modifications you do to your technique, from mouth position to fingering, will always depend on the advice of a tuner rather than on your own musical knowledge and expertise.

The visual references that the tuner points out to us act very similarly to the corrections a teacher shares with us, regarding the tune we play. While they might be well received and help us solve an immediate problem, they do not help us in the long run. If we are not able to develop our inner ear, we will always be depending on outside help to play our instrument. All students reading this, beware. The inner ear should be considered the main engine driving our ability to play in tune.

A well-developed musical inner ear gives us the capacity to recognize how a sound should sound based on the sound vibrations we detect and interpret in our brains. Our inner ears not only tell us how that note should sound in reference to the others that we hear at the same time (harmonic tuning) but also those in relation to those that are melodical (melodic tuning).

How can you educate your hearing?

I am sorry to tell you that there is no magic formula for the development of an educated musical ear. Depending on the innate capabilities of yourself as an individual, you might need to work more or less than others to train your auditory sense as a musician.

Before going into my musical ear training approach, I must share a few words about the saxophone itself. Since your instrument will be the main source of sound during your auditory education, it will be a central element of your training. It would be naïve to think that the quality of your saxophone won't have any impact over the development of your musical hearing. Even if you are just starting out, a good quality instrument will be your best ally. I insist that a good quality instrument is not necessarily the same as an expensive one. I am simply referring to an instrument that is good at doing what it was designed to do, producing the fully fleshed sounds of different musical notes.

Getting an instrument that isn't able to perform its rightful duty can be very problematic at the beginning. You will be exposing your novice ears to bad sounds. This can be especially harmful to young children who still don't have an understanding of what a good and bad sound is. For them, playing on a poorly made instrument comes with the risk of normalizing bad quality sound. In turn, their musical hearing abilities won't be able to draw accurate conclusions about sound. Nonetheless, getting used to hearing a bad sound, and being out of tune can make it difficult for older children and adults to interpret sounds properly.

To develop the ability to use our hearing to tune an instrument, we can divide our training into two main parts: training done without the instrument and training completed with the instrument. While I can't assign a precise percentage of importance to each of these tasks, I recommend devoting about 60% of your time to training without the saxophone and the remaining 40% to training with the saxophone.

Musical hearing training that is completed without the use of the saxophone is closely related to the study of musical language. Most people take at least one music-related class during their schooling, even if it's the only choir. Without a doubt, this basic musical training provides us with important notions and insights about the musical language, which can help us when we are approaching a new instrument such as the saxophone.

As part of your training, I encourage you to practice singing both alone and with others, listening to music, instrumental preferably, and analyzing sound. You can also watch saxophonist performers on the video to get better acquainted with its sound. This should be a habit that routinely accompanies us throughout our musical career. Later on, musical exposure will help us externalize our inner ear.

Training that is completed with the saxophone can be further divided into two different types: specific training and recording-listening of the practice exercises. Within the specific saxophone training, I propose practicing several music passages. As you play, each note should be listened to and tested, and not to move onto the next until you can determine that they are being played correctly.

You have to feel and internalize different sound fluctuations, which can also be perceived as sound waves. The better we become at identifying sound fluctuations when we listen to our playing, the more refined our musical hearing will become. Once we identify them, we must work at reducing these sound waves heard during notes as much as possible, so that sounds become uniform, full, and robust. Once no sound alterations are present, we will have successfully achieved our goal of playing in tune. On the contrary, identifying numerous sound fluctuations in a note's sound can indicate that we are still playing out of tune.

It is always highly recommended to try these tuning exercises under the guidance and instruction of a well-trained saxophonist instructor. When this option is not available, recording and listening to our own playing is a good method that will help us study sound and correct any issues that we were not able to appreciate at the moment. Try playing a saxophone solo, for example, recording it and listen to the recording later. Your analytical ear is going to start listening to the music in a detached way allowing you to evaluate melodic tuning more accurately.

In summary, we can affirm that the work of fine-tuning is directly related to a hearing capacity that we develop throughout our lives. That ability requires persistent and daily training that is not exclusive to practice on the actual saxophone. We must transfer this concept into our study sessions so that we can dedicate a proper amount of time to cultivating musical hearing and tuning abilities.

As you continue educating your hearing and perfecting your saxophones sound, it pays off to get to know your instrument in more detail. Get familiar with all of its individual peculiarities. Are there any notes that are not correctly toned? If so, what do you need to do to correct each of their tunings? Preferably try to answer these questions without the aid of a tuner. Only if you are not able to answer them based on your experience and skill, use a tuner device as an aid.

When you have otherwise failed to identify your tuning problems due to an underdeveloped musical ear, it is advisable to study in front of the tuner. This will allow you to draw pertinent conclusions and act accordingly.

We know, in general terms, that the saxophone has a certain set of note tuning characteristics. However, this changes considerably between the types of saxophone and can also vary depending on the brands.

The way to use the tuner as aid is to first play the note without looking at it and simply listen. If you are familiar with the sound characteristics of your instrument, you will be able to determine whether the sound is right or not. If you are struggling to listen, close your eyes, it can help you to hear better. Then do this again, but this time look at the tuner and observe if there is a problem and what that problem is. Doing so will do wonders to improve your sound and tuning awareness.

Other Training Approaches

Practicing with vowels is another method you can try to develop your musical ear for the purpose of tuning. To put into practice all the physical concepts that occur in the internal part of the mouth, we can help ourselves with the work using vowels. Mastering vowel sounds will undoubtedly be beneficial for developing a good saxophone sound since changing the pitch of the notes through the relaxation and contraction on the lower jaw muscles is related to sound quality.

You can also practice tuning your saxophone with the aid of another instrument. Exposure to other instrumental sounds serves to educate our hearing.

Tuning On The Saxophone

Learning to tune the saxophone is a long process that takes years to understand and execute. We must differentiate tuning the instrument with tuning in general, since the latter is much more complicated.

Our brain is continuously analyzing and comparing the sound that we emit with the other sounds that we listen to. This allows us to understand sound and educate our musical ear. By educating our ear, we will be able to know if we are emitting sounds that are tuned or not, and if those sounds are sharper or lower than they should be.

One of the most important skills that we have to learn in our musical lives as musicians in the art of tuning sounds. Regardless of whether we have good technique and are capable of playing more notes every day, the work of sound and tuning is vital to achieving our musical goals, and in turn, it is one of the most difficult things to achieve.

Tuning is a continuous process of listening to ourselves and interpreting our sounds based on our surroundings. When we learn to tune our sound properly, we are exhibiting our ability to adapt to different circumstances by overcoming technical difficulties or external difficulties.

We must clarify a number of simple concepts regarding tuning. The study with the tuner must be complementary to the work of comparison of sound intervals and identification of sounds that are out of tune. Using a tuner device, we will know how our instrument works and how it behaves, in normal conditions, with respect to its sound. The tuner behaves like a smoke alarm, which can instantly detect whether a note is out of tune or not and let us now accordingly. But in order to accomplish this, we must study with it under different conditions such as temperature and external humidity. The temperature greatly influences the tuning of the instrument. The saxophone is heated much more by the breathing air, increasing the ambient temperature even by 10 degrees. This is because of the density of the air.

The hot air from the column of wind does not vary the wavelength, nor the size, of the sound wave. Yet it does cause a change in the medium in which sound vibrates, which acquires a minimum degree of density. The lower the density of the air column, the faster its particles vibrate, and the louder the sound we hear. As it cools, the air contracts, acquiring a higher density, and the particles vibrate more slowly. This is why a cold wind instrument is low, and when warmed up, its pitch rises.

Other elements that affect tuning include the pressure of the air column and the materials with which we play, such as the type of mouthpiece and reeds.

The way in which we use the tuner when tuning our saxophone is very important. I am going to give you some general guidelines so that all this work is positive. Perform a good warm-up, since the temperature of the instrument influences the tuning as well as the pressure you exert with the mouthpiece.

When we are tuning, our notes end up being lower and sound more serious than they should. Therefore the appropriate correction would be to elevate the pitch by making the note sharper. The opposite occurs when we over the tune, and our sound is too high in its pitch.

In order to listen to the tuning, it is perhaps easier to start by listening to the sounds that are out of tune. When two notes are out of tune, the sound fluctuations or a beat produced by the shock of sound waves are heard. The more you can perceive this sound alteration, the more out of tune you are. When the sounds get closer to the correct tuning, the sound fluctuations become more spaced out and harder to perceive. The sound keeps on becoming more stable until it is uniform like a straight line. This is a clear indicator that a sound is completely tuned.

When we play with different dynamics, our tuning changes, it changes because we modify our pressure and quantity of air. As saxophonists, we must also become equipped to deal with this situation. For example, when blowing forte, we lower the pressure on the reed, and the sound drops. On the contrary, when we tighten the chin, the tuning goes up. Therefore, the need to practice tuning in different conditions, prioritizing sound quality is great and can be the work of many years.

Overview: How to correct sounds that are out of tune?

Here is an overview of what you should focus on to improve the sound and tune on the saxophone:

- Always look for a good sound and a good air column.

- Train the proper use of our respiratory system.

- Work with different saxophones and or instruments.

- Sing frequently and practice tuning with vowels.

- Adapt your mouth, air column, and larynx position, in different ways.

- Correct sounds that are out of tune by using tuning devices only as a last resort.

This laborious work of improving our sound will accompany us throughout our musical career, and it comes to reaffirming my theory that the most we saxophonists, or any musician, have to work with are two concepts: sound and tuning.

Chapter 8

How to Study A Musical Piece

Studying musical theory and practicing notes and exercises is necessary, but it is hardly any fun. In truth, no person is attracted to picking up a new instrument due to the fact that hours of practicing tedious, methodical scales and decoding  musical language are involved. What new students really want is to be able to play some of their favorite songs and musical pieces and share their advancement with friends and loved ones.

However, it is important to keep in mind that having a firm set of theoretical knowledge and practice playing notes and scales will help you better interpret songs on the saxophone. If, like most students, you are interested in starting to play some musical pieces, this section of the book is the best one to help you tackle the task. Here, we'll tackle the many different approaches one can take to study a musical passage with the saxophone. We'll go over a set of simple steps that will help you learn to play any musical passage with the saxophone, regardless of the difficulty of the song. Whether you are at a point where you simply want to play a beginner level song or move on to something more challenging, this information will help you achieve your goals. While you might need to adapt this methodology as you progress, it will provide you a strong foundation.

Before we get started, it is vital that we clarify some points. This chapter of the book will not tell you how to create a study plan for your entire saxophone learning journey. Giving you a set study schedule or specific methodology won't help you master a musical passage. Instead, we will focus on what approach you should take when tackling a new song or musical piece in order to master it as quickly and easily as possible.

At first, you should focus on deconstructing the notes in the song and going through them slowly. It is perfectly acceptable to practice without a compass at this stage. Move through the notes in a relatively slow fashion, verifying that you are getting the sounds right. The most important thing at first is to work on the execution of individual notes or small parts of the piece. Move forward in an orderly and structured fashion. Once you have a better grasp of the notes and their order, you can start improving your interpretation of the song by starting to look for musicality. Try to focus on the timing of the notes, but also con the connection that makes them weave and flow together. Listening to the song a few times and getting well acquainted with the rhythm can really help at this point.

Once you have run through the piece a few times and feel more confident with your advances, you should try to identify the most difficult passages in the piece or those that represent the biggest challenges to you. It is very important to identify and extract them. Work independently on these parts of the song. Practice them several times if necessary. Be patient throughout the process. Many times we insist on practicing through troubling passages in a fast or careless manner. Even if you feel frustrated when you can't get a part of the song right, try to remain calm and focused. Correcting and perfecting weak areas, even as a beginner, will save you a lot of trouble later and is always well worth it. To see true improvements you'll have to put in the time and effort. Only in this way will you be able to learn any musical piece correctly.

Once you have identified that most difficult passages, the next step you should take is to take them apart and study them in detail, you can do this by playing the passage several times per session, going through the notes slowly and cautiously. As you do this, make sure not to only focus on the correct fingering and proper breathing, but also try to find musicality. You can do this by mentally mapping the flow of the song in your mind. Are there any high or low points? Is the rhythm cheerful, sad, or somber? You can even try humming the song a few times to get a feel for the general direction to take when you play. As you practice, keep all of these elements in mind.

I often follow this technique in my own practice, even after years of playing the sax. This approach allows me to break down the passages and practice them slowly, giving me time to think and listen. Without much effort, but simply true repetition and focused practice, I often find myself memorizing entire musical pieces. What's best is that it's not only the basics of the piece that remains sealed in my mind but also the rhythm and melody.

Looping Notes When Playing Songs

All music is made out of different notes, linking together to produce melodies. The link between the notes should be smooth and precise, so as to not alter the true nature of the song. When you are just learning a new musical piece, it is important that you pay close attention to the note links and work to make these small transitions as smooth and natural as possible. When I detect that the link between two notes is not cOrrect or isn't being properly executed, I make sure to practice the note transitions over and over until the right rhythm and melody are achieved. At first, during practice, I play the note loops on repeat at a slow pace. Once I feel more confident with the melody, I gradually speed up my playing, working up to the actual pace of the song.

There are many reasons why you might be struggling with certain note loops. For some, it is the quick fingering changes that pose the real challenge. Others find it more difficult to understand rhythm and pace, which can cause them to change from one note to another too abruptly or slowly. We must isolate the problem and practice the note transition until the loop becomes natural.

One example where I have applied this technique to improve note linking is in the D sharp link with the F. In this transition, a hook-like effect can be heard in some specific musical pieces. At first, I struggled to reproduce this effect in the transition of the notes. First,

I thought the problem was the intonation of the note. If this is something you might be struggling with in your note transitions, it is very helpful to change the octave in which the passage is played.

A different method you could try is to change up your note articulation. Articulation refers to the musical parameters that determine how a sounds and includes the duration of the sound as well as the shape of its attack and then of its decay. Without a doubt, articulation variations are among the most fruitful changes that can be made when studying a difficult passage. It is like learning to travel from one city to another on different paths. For example, you could try playing a particular passage with both a staccato and tenuto articulation styles. Staccato notes are shortened and not attached to one another, creating abrupt breaks between notes. On the contrary, with tenuto articulation, notes are held for longer, for their full length. In woodwind instruments, these variations are made using the tongue, since tongue movements can be used to break the flow of air.

A transition between two notes when long and loud can be challenging to achieve, so trying a more chopped articulation is a good approach. Once you have been able to master the transition, you can start varying the articulation and lengthening the notes until you are able to work up to the desired effect. This will also give you time to memorize and adjust the fingering to develop more agile movements. In some cases, it is clumsy fingers that can be keeping you from properly transition between notes.

Another approach we can take to work through a difficult transition is practicing the passage with different rhythms. Changing the rhythm can help because, at times, the real problem students face when trying to reproduce a specific rhythm in a melody is a difficulty to pinpoint to follow a set rhythm. If you are still not seeing a noticeable improvement after trying to work through the song and different note links using the previous suggestions, I often suggest continuing the process by trying to change up the rhythm.

To do this, simply play the musical passage while applying a different rhythm, as if it were a different melody. While this won't help you increase precision in the execution of the piece, it will help you get over any struggles you might be having with the rhythm and be able to better concentrate on the notes and their transitions. The more rhythm changes you try, and the more times you practice, the better the results you will obtain when you try to play the original version. You can even try changing up the compass and the tempo or add a swing to sound.

To best adjust your timing and tempo, you might feel compelled to help yourself with the metronome and possibly even make further improvements with a tuner or another instrument that can help you polish off your sound.

Memorization is another important tool that will help you put together musical pieces with ease. As you begin to practice difficult passages, aim to memorize them first, rather than to get sound right from the first try. The last thing you want to do when playing a challenging set of notes is to be stressing about looking at the music sheet to figure out what comes next. Knowing the notes by heart will give you a stronger level of confidence that will allow you to concentrate on more important aspects of the piece. Being able to review a passage with your eyes closed helps you best internalize it and learn it.

Finally, if you are truly not making any progress despite your best efforts, it might be time to take a short break. Yes, you read it right. I am advising you to take a break from practicing.

At times, we are simply experiencing a block or have unrelated emotional tension and are unable to put together a musical passage successfully, despite good technique and motivation. Insisting on everything being resolved in one day, in this type of situation, will only result in unnecessary frustration. Sometimes even two or three days will not be enough to work through a particularly challenging passage, and that is okay. Keep in mind that you do not speed learning the saxophone but are on a long term learning path.

If I am starting to feel stressed and frustrated, my practice regularly suffers. When this happens, I simply move on to something else and resume my studies the next day. Eventually, the difficulties can always be worked out. Speed is never a measure of success for a musician, but rather improvement of sound and knowledge. It doesn't matter if achieving such improvements takes up a long time.

Speed is the one thing you should be the least worried about, which is the reason why I mention it last. Some musical pieces demand great speed in certain passages. Often this is the main reason why students struggle to play complete musical pieces with smooth note transitions. Trying to meet speed requirements can easily make us slip up unintentionally as we play.

When you work in a more advanced passage, first, you must follow all the previous recommendations to improve your execution. Once you have done this, you can begin to work on increasing the playing speed up to the speed you would need to play it during a performance. For that, I recommend using the metronome and arming yourself with patience for practice.

If, at first, you do not succeed, do not obsess. Remember that rest is important too. Start playing as slow as you need to go to play the piece or passage with accuracy. Then gradually increase the speed until its perfect.

Chapter 9

Using A Metronome

The topic of the metronome is one of great controversy within the musical world. Musicians constantly debate whether this instrument should be used to study music and whether its use is actually correct or not. Based on my own experience, I always recommend the use of a metronome during the first stages of learning the saxophone.

The use of the metronome or its variants, such as recorded play-along tracks or musical rhythms, allows the beginner musician to correctly synchronize their internal timing and tempo to improve their playing. Of course, the development of an internal sense of tempo is not done by simply listening to a metronome, but by listening to a lot of varied music, playing in a group, feeling and understanding music, singing, etc. What's more, I strongly recommend using the metronome when you are experimenting with playing along with different musical rhythms. This will make its use more effective and fun.

We must use the metronome as if it were an accompanying instrument and become as aware of it during our practice as we would be of a fellow musician during a group performance. Alternating between playing with and without a metronome is also important so that we can get a better understanding of how it works and notice the differences in playing with its aid and without. Some cases in which I recommend using the metronome include:

- To keep track of your breathing throughout a musical piece

- When you are studying sound, note articulation, and saxophone sound effects

- When you are uncertain about and want to verify your timing and your tempo for a specific musical passage

- When studying techniques with scales and arpeggios, always doing it first at slow speeds and increasing the speed progressively

- When studying and practicing a playing technique at different speeds

- When you are working on a difficult passage that you have already memorized, but you are looking to polish with great precision (for example, when preparing for public performance)

On the other hand, I recommend avoiding the use of the metronome under this other set of circumstances:

- Stop using the metronome immediately if you have started to believe that you cannot play without it. This is a clear sign that you are developing a dependency on this tool, which can become an important roadblock to you as a saxophonist.

  In technical or musical passages in your early stages of study, i.e., when you are playing the passage for the first time or just getting started with memorization. Remember that the metronome will simply help us accurately adjust our timing and tempo and is, in turn, useful for the polishing of a piece, not for the actual learning process.

- Do not use the metronome when playing in public and during any performance with an audience.

Nowadays, digital metronomes are widely available and can even be set on a smartphone with the surge of diverse mobile applications for musicians. Therefore if you want to use it or could benefit from using it to perfect your tempo, you have no excuse to put it off. My personal advice is that if you are studying saxophone, start using it as soon as possible. At the early stages, you must learn how to internalize timing and tempo, and this tool will be your best asset. As you start to understand the flow of music, you can start steering away from its use.

Conclusion

Music is the art of combining sounds, respecting harmony, and rhythm. Musical organization and execution requires a significant amount of mental work and can even be considered a complex mental exercise. Still, it is a very enriching and worthy passion to take on for both the mind and for the social and personal sphere. There are even some who believe that the practice of music helps people to develop a feeling of spirituality. One can see this when analyzing the ideas of some recognized people in history. For example, we can take a look at the following thought, "Next to the Word of God, music deserves the highest praise. The gift of language combined with the gift of song was given to man so that he should proclaim the Word of God through Music," according to Martin Luther. This goes to show how strongly people believe in the link between music and spiritual connection.

Music students who constantly practice improving their technique and performance enjoy numerous benefits on top of a growing ability to play an instrument. It doesn't matter whether you are looking to learn the saxophone as a hobby, to meet a personal goal, or as a part of a journey for professional musical development. The time you invest in learning and the dedication you put into its study will result in a wide range of benefits that extend beyond the area of musical expertise.

The purpose of this book is to be able to introduce any beginner interested in learning a new musical instrument, the saxophone, to the basics necessary to successfully complete this task, as well as to expose them to all the benefits that learning the sax entails.

Playing a musical instrument requires specific skills to master technique and execution. Some people find it easier to get started than others. This has led many to believe that one can be born with innate musical talent. Today many find themselves asking whether the musical ability is an innate quality or whether it is the product of intensive practice. Unfortunately, this very question acts as a roadblock for many, since an apparent lack of innate musical expertise can discourage students from trying to learn and improve.

In reality, there is little evidence to back up that a person is born with a determined set of musical skills from birth. That is not to deny that certain requirements are necessary to be able to perform an instrument successfully. Among them are drive and discipline to practice, dedication, theoretical knowledge, and, finally, but most importantly, love or passion for music and the instrument.

It is vital that we not only focus on immediate musical results but the complete development of one as a musician. By practicing these exercises and starting to play musical pieces, you will discover certain benefits that will gradually leave a mark on your life. For example, you may notice certain changes in your mental agility. This is due to a phenomenon studied by several specialists in neuropsychology, in which they observed that music has a great influence on the plasticity of the brain. For this reason, it is hypothesized that playing a musical instrument can possibly help to improve cognitive performance.

At the beginning of your learning journey, you will start to memorize musical notes and start to recognize them through their sounds. This helps strengthen the senses and the brain's ability to adapt and respond to different environmental cues. Musicians have even been shown in several studies to have a larger cerebral cortex and an increased amount of white matter in the brain. White matter acts as an information transmitter and coordinator between different parts of the mind. The development of this area makes connections faster and easier to achieve.

At the same time, studying music helps the student to improve the way they deal with problems of abstraction. As you become skilled in working with the timing of the music, and precisely adjusting the duration of each musical note, you will be activating different parts of your brain that are engaged in solving numerical problems, for example when solving a mathematical equation.

The musician also regularly integrates theoretical and practical knowledge, which must be used at the same time when music is played. This integration of information and skill uniquely exercises the brain, increasing its ability to process information and its response capacity.

By playing the saxophone, you will also find a healthy outlet to communicate your emotions. Musical improvisation, composition, and interpretation have been used since the beginning of time as a form of artistic and emotional expression. You can communicate simple and complex messages through melodic sound alone. Different rhythms, genres, and playing styles all contribute to the communicative nature of music.

If you are not big on writing or talking about your feelings but would still like to find an outlet for communication and relaxation, the saxophone is a great tool to consider. Furthermore, the sax is an instrument where mental ability is of the utmost importance, which means that your mind will always be engaged and improving, no matter how much you have advanced in the art.

Compared to other instruments, you will discover that playing the saxophone also offers many musical advantages, especially in the flexibility and freedom it can give the musician. Some instruments out there have a sound that is specifically suited for a limited number of musical genres and songs. Unlike these instruments, the saxophone doesn't have a niched down sound. Despite its unique characteristics, the instrument can adapt to nearly any musical piece from jazz to Latin rhythms. This is partly due to the voice-like nature of the instrument, which can mimic human singing patterns.

It is for this reason that saxophones and their unique sounds can be found in almost all musical genres and different decades. No matter what type of music you enjoy or want to play, you can find a way to integrate your instrument with great results. This explains why saxophone sound is included in songs that range from classical to electronic.

Another benefit of the saxophone is that while it integrates smoothly with other instruments, its use is not limited to group performances. In fact, there are many successful and famous saxophonists who have gained recognition for their individual performances. This means that even if you don't have any musician friends and are practicing completely on your own, you will never feel limited in your practice or musical piece interpretation.

Additionally, the saxophone is an instrument that will not only improve your musical abilities but also help you improve one of the most basic physical functions of your body, which is breathing. As we studied throughout this book, breathing exercises tailored to improve your breathing and boost lung capacity are essential in the study of the saxophone. The development of breathing capacity and control is essential since, without it, the musician couldn't play extended notes or passages without running out of breath. For wind musicians, breathing can become as important - if not more important -than musical theory, since it determines largely how notes played will sound. Practicing breathing exercises and frequently playing the saxophone helps you become more aware of your diaphragm and respiratory movements. This, in turn, leads to increased breathing capacity and can help you improve your health and even fitness performance in your daily life.

As mentioned earlier, the sax is also considered an easy instrument to learn due to its modern origin and easily located note keys. You will find that finger placement on the saxophone is a very natural feeling and easy to get used to. The lightweight nature of beginner-friendly saxophones like the Alto further increases its approachability.

Surprisingly a lot of young students are intimidated by the sophisticated appearance of the saxophone. Its long body and metallic finish and the presence of an abundance of interestingly shaped keys mistakenly lead many to believe that the saxophone is very difficult to play. It is only when they venture into learning the instrument that these students realize that the notes and scales are relatively easy to master and that with dedication progressing and growing as a saxophone player is a doable feat. It is important that you understand that all instruments require some effort, but that the saxophone is not especially complex or difficult. The sooner you understand this fact, the more motivated you will feel to pick up a saxophone and start learning this instrument now!

Best of all, once you get the hang of the instrument, you will be happy to find out that the saxophone has an extensive repertoire of great pieces of different difficulties. This will give you many opportunities to experiment and become the musician you have always wanted to be.

Learning to play the saxophone is now easier than ever because there are so many good quality saxophones available that can be purchased at a lower cost. Additionally, in today's world, learning resources abound both online and offline. You no longer have to depend one hundred percent on an expensive instructor to be able to master the saxophone. In fact, you can use resources like this book, online videos and sheet music to do a lot of the learning on your own.

Although the saxophone might have a bad reputation as an instrument that is challenging or difficult to play, it is actually one of the easiest instruments to learn due to its recent introduction and conveniently designed keys. If you want to learn to play this wonderful instrument, this book is the best guide you can have to instruct you through the first stages. As you move past the contents of this book, you can always refer back to it when the need arises.

Printed in Great Britain
by Amazon

76425946R00071